THE REAL HOWARDS' WAY

WRITTEN BY
CLIVE BROOKS

ILLUSTRATED BY
DAVID ELLERY

Published by Milestone Publications
62 Murray Road, Horndean, Portsmouth, Hants PO8 9JL
Published by arrangement with BBC Books, a division of BBC Enterprises Ltd

Design Brian Iles

Typeset by Monitor, Hayling Island
Printed and bound in Great Britain by
RJ Acford, Chichester, West Sussex

Brooks, Clive
The real Howards' Way.
1. Bursledon Region (Hampshire)——Social
life and customs
I. Title II. Ellery, David
942.2'772 DA690.B95/

ISBN 1-85265-109-1

Contents

This book is dedicated to my wife, Amanda, and my Mum.

I would like to thank everyone who has assisted in the preparation of this book, including the 'locals', Denaise Photographic Services, Hythe, for the photographic printing, Amanda Little my agent, and in particular Nicholas Pine, of Milestone Publications, for making it all possible.

Clive Brooks *Southampton, 1987*

Introduction

The Hamble river is known to yachtsmen throughout the world. It is the most popular yachting harbour on the whole of the south coast and, in summer, it's an almost impenetrable forest of masts. Amidst this nautical scene, recently peeped the prying eyes of a BBC camera crew. The leafy lanes of Old Bursledon and its beautiful houses suddenly became a leisure location for millions of people, throughout the length and breadth of the country. Did this result in a problem for the tiny village? Was there suddenly a never ending traffic jam in the narrow lanes? No! Those millions of people visited the area regularly without even leaving their own favourite armchairs, via the hub of family entertainment, the television set.

Each week, wherever you lived, you could lose yourself for almost an hour in the yachting world, by following the fortunes, and otherwise, of the Howard family in the saga that became known to all as the hugely successful HOWARDS' WAY. As I write this, the cameras are set to return to produce what will eventually be moulded into a third series. No viewer can have failed to notice, and admire, the wonderful backdrop that the area provides to the series. But do the on-screen locations really exist? And if they do, where are they? Who owns them? And is the series really true to life?

This book will, I hope, provide you with all the answers, and a great deal more besides, giving you the opportunity of taking your own trip down Howards' Way, and reliving some of the drama and excitement for yourself, through the eyes of the camera, and the local characters themselves.

The River Hamble — a forest of masts

A familiar scene providing a perfect backdrop to the series.

Bursledon
The Tarrant Transformation

The fictional village of Tarrant, around which the majority of the series revolves, is in fact the beautiful conservation area of Old Bursledon. It finally arrived at this real-life name over a period of seven hundred years. In its time, it has been called Brixedone, Brixenden, Bristleden, and Bussleton. Forests once lined the banks of the nearby River Hamble, providing shelter, especially at Burseldon, which became the site of shipyards from the age of the 'wooden walls'. In fact, the Royal Navy's first Man o'War, the *St George* was built at Bursledon, and launched on St George's Day in 1338 by King Edward III. Now the wooden designs have, much to the consternation of Jack Rolfe of the fictional 'Mermaid Yard', been·replaced by fibreglass constructions.

The Howard's House

Several beautiful properties were 'requisitioned' to feature in the television series. Most notable of these is Bondfield House. Situated in Kew Lane in the heart of the Old Bursledon conservation area, it was recently on the market for £225,000. This lovely house, built in 1896, was, for a few weeks, the home of the 'Howards'. However, for the remainder of its time, it is the residence of the Mason family.

The five bedroomed property stands in almost three and a half acres and can easily be recognised by the large conservatory on the side. This was featured in the scene where Abbey realised that Freyer was her father in the

Bondfield House — home to both Masons and Howards

The Mason family seen here with their numerous pets

second series. I asked Mrs Mason if they were living in the house during the filming?

"We'd just moved in, about four or five days before. It was a tremendous shock. We were told by the previous owners that the BBC were using the property, and that they were hoping to use it again for the second series. They were very nice, and very considerate. They didn't film any interiors here. They were all built in a studio. However, they did have to come into the house for the wedding scene between Lynne and Claude. Lynne (Tracey Childs) had to change into the wedding dress, and had to make her way through our tea chests and everything else. It was quite chaotic when they came in with the dresses and make up artists".

The wedding took place up at nearby St Leonard's church and was, by all accounts, quite an occasion for the locals of Bursledon, as well as the viewers.

"The church scenes were unbelievable!" exclaimed Mrs Mason. "When they wanted a shot of someone moving their hand or something, it would often take about three hours. We were actually sitting in the congregation. We weren't allowed to move or do anything, so everyone was very tense all the time, and it really took a long time. We couldn't believe it when we saw it on the television, it only seemed to last a minute or so and that was it."

Nothing much was changed for the filming at Bondfield House, apart from in the porch, where the BBC brought in some boards with instant wallpaper on. These were placed in front of the walls to cover everything. In addition, some extra plants were placed in the conservatory".

Going back to the wedding scene, I asked if it was all over at the house very quickly...

"No, when they did the wedding scene, they were in and out of the front door about thirty times, but they didn't actually shoot inside. They just had Lynne Howard walking down the stairs to make sure that the timing of the shots taken from outside was realistic."

The filming at Bondfield for the second series was broken up, with a fortnight between sessions, and the filming lasting

Bondfield House — set in nearly three and a half acres of ground

The large conservatory played an important part

for about four days altogether, in half day sessions. However, the wedding took the whole day. The BBC's attention to detail was very much in evidence during the Bondfield House sessions. At one point, they erected a large marquee in the garden which was treated to no more than a fleeting glimpse in the finished production. From Mrs Mason's point of view, it was perhaps worth it because it offered the best view in the whole series of her house.

Being newcomers to the area, I wondered if the Mason's had been able to gauge their neighbour's reaction to the excitement next door.

"We don't really hear very much from one side," said Mrs Mason, "But the others were very friendly, and quite interested. As we'd only been here a few days, we didn't know them really, but we did see them peeping through their windows. Now we're quite close to them, and so next time they'll probably come and actually watch. I think that, as they'd seen it all happen before during the filming for the first series, they knew what to expect much more than we did!"

I asked Mrs Mason and her daughters Emma and Lucy what their reaction was to the completed series, and whether they'd watched before getting involved.

"I hadn't seen any of Howards' Way before we got involved," said Mrs Mason, "When the cast were here, I didn't know them from the crew, I hadn't a clue. Having seen how it's filmed now, you get a different perspective on the whole thing."

LUCY: "They didn't bring this house into it until the end really, so we weren't that interested because it wasn't showing any clips, but towards the end we were really glued to it. I think that the storyline improved towards the end of the second series. The other episode's scripts varied enormously from good to bad."

"Yes," agreed Emma, "The first series was better than the second. It seemed more real. I think that they got a bit carried away in the second."

"I think that they must have spent most of the extra

The porch of Bondfield House was featured in several episodes

budget in the second series on clothes," pointed out Mrs Mason with a smile.

Living in Bursledon, in the midst of the yachting world, it seemed probable that the 'real life Howards' would be keen on getting afloat.

"We're going to take some sailing courses," said Lucy. "We've been out a couple of times with friends already. I think that's probably the best way to get into it. You meet so many people around here that you just have to jump at the opportunity."

The BBC's extremely high standards of efficiency and pre-planning were much in evidence throughout the filming, and were mentioned by everyone that I spoke to, but sometimes unforeseen things happen...

"It was funny because if an aeroplane went over then they would say, 'right, hold,' they were very professional in that respect. Most things were taken dozens of times, and by the time we watched the finished thing we knew every single word."

LUCY: "One time, it was very difficult because lots of planes were coming over and it was getting late and they needed to finish it. Something kept on going wrong and they were getting a bit ratty about it. Then, to make matters worse, all our dogs would charge out onto the lawn."

MRS MASON: "Everything would stop for food. They were very strict with the food breaks. They all looked forward to that, and the catering was brilliant. They made the breaks one of the main points of the day. I think that it's something to do with the unions."

LUCY: "Yes, we were invited to go around with them. They let us go onto their special coach at lunchtime. There's a visitors one and Maurice, who's Tom, was so sweet. We had lunch with them and got really well looked after."

EMMA: "I thought they'd be sort of stand-offish, and when they first came to talk to us we we're a bit awestruck, but then you build up a relationship, and then when they came back, it was good fun. They're just ordinary people really."

Bondfield House — from the top of the rear steps

Bondfield House — very much a family home

This is all very well, but do they resemble their on-screen characters?

LUCY: "Some of the cast are like the characters that they portray, like Ken Masters. He's really sort of smooth, but Leo is totally different. He's really a joker, and very friendly. Also, Tom is in fact much nicer than you might think in real life.

MRS MASON: "Yes, they are very nice. We were invited onto their boat at the end of the filming for a party. It was one of the ferries. It just pottered round. We had very good food and lots to drink. It was very kind of them to ask us."

I noticed that, in the estate agents particulars of the house, it was mentioned that it was used in Howards' Way. Could this have influenced the Mason's decision to purchase, one way or the other?

"When we were first sent the particulars I just tore them up!" Laughed Mrs Mason. "For one thing it was overpriced and also I thought, 'Well, I don't really want to live around there'. But here we are, right in the middle of it after all."

So what do the Mason's friends think of their involvement with the nationally successful series?

EMMA: "My friends tease me at school. It's amazing how it's got around, because when we go back to Yorkshire where we used to live and visit our tennis club, a lot of our friends say, 'Your house is the one used in Howards' Way, isn't it?' They quip 'how's Howard', and things like that. It's amazing how people get to know about it, but they don't treat me any differently."

LUCY: "It's the same at work. They know I live in Bursledon, so they say 'is it near the house used in Howards' Way?', and they ask what ours is called. I tell them it's Bondfield House, and they suddenly realise that it WAS used. Within seconds it was the office talking point. Suddenly, it becomes a bit of a joke, as if it makes us any different!"

I asked Emma if she thought that any of the characters from the series would really fit into everyday village life?

"In the first series, the characters they played would have

The patio and conservatory at the rear of the property

The idyllic Hamble, could anywhere else really have been used?

done, but now I think they're all too smart, and far too sophisticated for this place!"

Jan Howard's boutique became an important feature of the second series, but what about the designs themselves, are they really wearable?

"Some of them are very nice," grinned Lucy, "others are really terrible. But I like some of the clothes that Jan herself wears."

Being what I supposed could be termed a 'local', I personally feel that the series simply wouldn't have been the same had it been filmed elsewhere. I wondered if my views were shared by Mrs Mason, or not. . .

"I think it would be as good, and probably wouldn't make much difference. I think there are lots of places around Devon and Cornwall that could have been used to equally good effect. It's just a case of good photography, and picking out the best shots of an area.

It's hard to believe that a major series such as Howards'

Way is run on a tight budget, but with this in mind, then Mrs Mason's last comment doesn't come as too much of a surprise:

"We were only paid for inconvenience. But I can't remember the exact figure. Their recurring big joke is, 'This is the BBC, not ITV'. I guess that all the independent companies must have more money to spend on their productions, surprisingly!"

The Real Mermaid Yard

Even if it had wanted to, Bursledon couldn't have made a better job of concealing the real Mermaid Yard. Yes, it does exist and yes, it is a small riverside family run boatyard. But no, it isn't really called the Mermaid at all. Oh no, it sports a much stranger name than that, which initally appears far from nautical; it is The Elephant Boatyard.

Actually, when you delve back into history, the name does in fact have a solid nautical foundation, and quite a distinguished one at that. It is named after Nelson's flagship from the Battle of Copenhagen. *HMS Elephant,* as it was called, was built on the site in 1786. It was one of the 74-gun ships of the line that became the standard Naval design. From its introduction to the service during the seven years war, (1755-63), until after the Napoleonic Wars which ended in 1815, more than 200 served with the Royal Navy. The design owed it's success to it being the smallest practical sized ship to carry a full battery of 32-pounders on two decks. At one stage, the ship was in the command of Captain Francis William Austen, the brother of the famous Hampshire novelist, Jane Austen.

HMS Elephant was designed by Sir Thomas Slade, built by George Parson of Bursledon in February 1783, and then subsequently launched in August 1786. She formed one of the 'Arrogant' class. The ship was finally taken apart in 1868 after 82 years service, and it is thought that much of her

The 'real' sign in the road above the yard

Boats moored in the yard as seen in many an episode

timber still survives today in old barns and buildings around Hampshire.

There is a house to commemorate George Parsons in Lands End Road called Parson's Plot. When he failed to obtain renewal of his lease on the boatyard site, he moved his sheds, equipment and even his men across to the other side of the river at nearby Warsash. Here he built cottages and an Inn called the Sun. This has become the present Rising Sun, on the quay.

The coming of the railway to Bursledon at the turn of the century considerably altered the access to the river, and the old shipbuilding yards on the Bursledon shore which had to be supplied with tremendous loads of prime oak trees from the Forest of Bere and other sources. Many of the old shipbuilder's cottages remain, outwardly unchanged, and Bursledon pool must have formed a tranquil setting for the teams of carthorses and carters, and the toilers at the sawpits, as the shipwrights shaped and faired countless tons of sweet smelling oak.

Shipbuilding had long been a major industry up and down the Hamble River. In St Leonard's church there are memorials to shipbuilders George Parsons and Philomen Ewer. These indicate the high esteem that shipbuilders were held in those days.

But back to the Mermaid (or should I say Elephant?). It is, in real life, owned by the Richardson family, and there's not a Timber Tom, or Jack Rolfe in sight. There is no public access to the yard, but splendid views can be obtained from the Hamble River itself, where it can easily be picked out from amongst the array of masts, by its large circular white logo, depicting the figure of a silhouetted black elephant.

The Elephant yard was founded in 1952 by Mike Richardson. It operates as a traditional yacht yard, and has built up an enviable reputation over the years for repairs in wood and GRP (Glass reinforced plastic), as well as offering fitting out and other services to both racing and cruising yachts. The yard has, in addition to its servicing, been involved in the construction of around forty yachts, both sail

The large elephant sign above the door of the main workshop

The Elephant Boat Yard — particularly picturesque when viewed from the river

and power. Many of these have been traditionally built in wood, and range in size from 24 to 55 ft.

The successes of racing yachts built in the yard include the 1979 yacht of the year; Doug Peterson's ½ ton *Green Dragon,* and the one ton *Dragon* of Ed Dubois, which represented Britain twice in the Admiral's Cup, most notably in 1981 as a member of the winning team. In addition, *Hurrycane,* another one tonner, designed by Peter Norlin won the Britannia Cup in 1984. These yachts have all got one thing in common; they were all built from Western Red Cedar on spruce laminated frames using modern glues and epoxy resins.

But yachts aren't all that the Elephant is capable of constructing, and this is demonstrated by the building of two 30ft steam launches. One was of traditional design, complete with stern cabin and funnel. The other was of modern power, sporting a steam turbine, and flash steam boiler designed by Dr Moulton, of 'Mini' motor car suspension fame.

There was much celebration in 1986 on the occasion of the 200th anniversary of the launch of *HMS Elephant,* (on the 24th of August 1786 to be exact), but 1986 was to be doubly memorable for the yard, as it became the centre of attention countrywide as the Mermaid yard. I asked Tom Richardson how the BBC first came to approach him with a view to filming there. . .

"Bob Fisher, the BBC's technical adviser to the series, had been approached to find a Yard on the south coast. He knew of several that might fit the bill, one of which was ours. He came down on a preliminary visit with the producer Gerry Glaister, some 15 months before they started filming the series. They both agreed that this was the site that they would like to use".

Filming at the boatyard was divided into two separate sessions. The first being about a week long, and the second about five days. Luckily, the yard is effectively split into two with a man-made creek. Shooting was arranged so that the normal boatyard work could continue on one side, whilst

Bob Fisher — in many ways a key figure to the series

the filming took place on the other. It was all done following the main spring rush, and so it didn't cause too much disruption to Tom's busy work schedules.

The yard must have been precisely what the BBC were seeking, as no major changes were required, and everything exists exactly as we see it on the screen. The BBC were even able to use boats that happened to be hauled out, for their background shots, and thus work unobtrusively for most of the time, while life went on around them, serving to add even more realism to the scenes. In fact, some of the yard's employees were sometimes featured in the footage simply going about their work. I wonder who were acting the most — the characters, or the boatyard workers?

Jack Rolfe's boatyard office exists at the Elephant, and is in fact Tom Richardson's headquarters. It's a converted boat, with the wooden offices perched on the decks. However, to avoid any disturbance, and to gain more scope for camera angles, the internal office shots were produced in the Pebble Mill studios in Birmingham.

I asked Tom if he lent the BBC a hand in any technical matters:

"I helped out with some of the dialogue in scripts that were used in the yard scenes. Obviously, we were very keen that they had all of the terminology right, because it could reflect on us if they didn't", he said.

The rivalry between the wooden and GRP boats seems, in real life, to be much less intense than the way we see it portrayed in the series. There are traditionalists around, and perhaps Tom Richardson could be considered as one of them, believing that quality should on no account be blatantly sacrificed for production line mass markets. In fact, the original *Barracuda of Tarrant* used in the series was built in cedar WOOD!! It was the plug, (or mould) for the production version called the *Barracuda 45* now being built by Sadler Yachts. It's amusing to think that 14 million people have been watching what they think is a revolutionary GRP boat, (which the production model is) when it is in fact built of wood, using modern methods. It's also surprising to learn

Inside the main workshop

The man-made creek within the yard

Work in progress

that the BBC were actually filming parts of the construction of the original *Barracuda* for the series.

I thought that perhaps the yard had been named the Mermaid due to the fact that a man-o-war of that name was built in the nearby New Forest's ancient Bucker's Hard shipyards, but apparently this is no more than a coincidence, as Tom Richardson thinks that it was simply 'picked from a hat' so to speak.

I wondered if the yard's new-found fame had produced a direct positive affect on orders, and whether customers did actually realise that it had been featured;

"We do find that some people arrive, and suddenly realise that it is the yard that was used in the series", said Tom. "They do a double take, and think they've seen it all somewhere before. But I think that it's rather nice that we get people on our reputation rather than through what is, after all, a soap opera".

There are a good many yards within close proximity to each other on the River Hamble, which at first glance

The Mermaid/Elephant yard office

Barracuda of Tarrant

provide the setting for a hot-bed of intense inter-yard rivalry and competition. Happily however, this doesn't seem to be the case at all these days;

"Up until about 1965, before the so-called yachting boom, there were fewer yachts being built, and it was difficult to start and run a boatyard from scratch. Nowadays of course, times have changed and there are plenty of customers for everyone. Inter-yard rivalry has, as a result, to all intents and purposes, disappeared."

During the first series, Jack Rolfe's Brother in Law returned from Australia, claiming that the Yard was his. The resulting court case went in Jack's favour, and so his Brother in Law took the law into his own hands and tried to get rid of Jack by arranging for a little accident on a yacht. The scene where the boat blew up and sank was very convincing, and a credit to the special effects department. They built a false deck out of balsa wood with an explosive charge underneath it. The boat was protected by steel plates. Under the hull they had a box with driftwood inside which exploded simultaneously. Hatch boards, etc, were all built out of lightweight material to fly out of the cockpit. Also, a sea cock below the waterline was opened to allow the boat to semi-sink. There was one poor guy down below who had to operate all that lot.

To keep things like this running smoothly, the BBC co-ordinate a shooting schedule with the Elephant yard. This details what shots they want to take, and where they want to take them. It also shows what days they would like to be present. All this provides a very good idea of what's actually occurring, and unless something horrendous happens with the weather, they apparently usually managed to keep to schedule. A fact that is very important to avoid the shooting running over budget.

In real life, launchings at the yard are very lavish affairs, with up to 100 people present, and the champagne flowing freely. This is especially true if it's a one-off boat. The yard is smothered with bright bunting, and it's considered by everyone to be a very important occasion. I asked why;

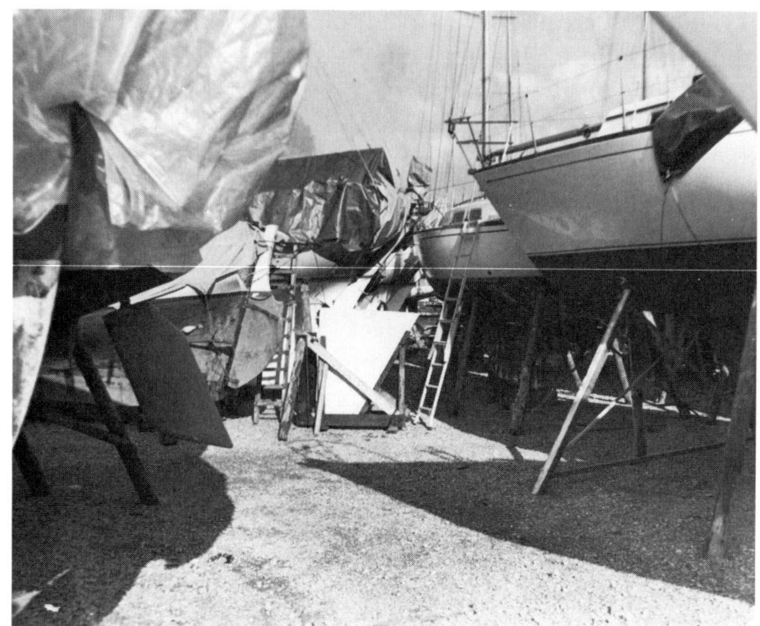

Many boats are out of the water awaiting or undergoing maintenance

The ideal location for Jack Rolfe's business

"The thing about the wooden boats that we build is that they have personalities. Back through maritime history, people have always talked about one-off yachts and ships as individuals, rather than just 'things'. With such a boat, that's been built especially for you, it's a very exciting occasion and we like to make it as memorable as we possibly can."

The majority of Howards' Way's weekly audience probably don't know a spinnaker from a genoa, and so the series will, whatever the BBC do, seem authentic. However, the director and his technical advisers have been at pains to get everything right, as far as possible. But did the completed episodes satisfy the critical eye of Tom, who's spent his whole life in the boatbuilding industry?

"I think the sailing scenes were very good", he said. "Of course, I would have liked to have seen more of them. I think that the yard has come in for such an incredibly hard time, that it would be difficult to keep a business going in the circumstances that our heroes have to put up with. As soaps go, I would much rather have it than an American one. It's certainly got more to it."

Boats of the Series

As Tom Howard tries to pick up the pieces from the Lynnette catamaran sinking, which was the culmination of the second series, I decided to find out whether there really was a 'Lynnette', and for that matter, a 'Barracuda' and a 'Flying Fish' as well. It didn't take long to find out that there was.

Do you remember the scenes in which Lynn Howard (played by Tracey Child) battled bravely away against the elements during her solo Atlantic crossing, in a successful attempt to prove the seaworthiness of the new Barracuda yacht? With the series on such a slim budget, travelling with the yacht across the Atlantic to film its triumphant arrival in New York harbour was out of the question. It was all carried out very sneakily in the cold murky waters of the Solent.

One difficulty was that of producing an authentic mid-Atlantic swell in the calm waters. This was solved by using six boats to circle the Barracuda and whip up the waves, together with two further craft armed with water cannons. They fired freezing cold Solent water all over Tracey who, despite two layers of heavy weather gear, shivered in front of the cameras for four hours. But has it deterred her from sailing? "I'm hooked!" she was reported to have said!

But what of New York harbour? Well, a sleepy little jetty was successfully persuaded to resemble it for the scenes. It's amazing what a few accents and a horde of photographers can do, isn't it? The last time that so much excitement was

The pontoon, which became America!

Tony Castro — "Barracuda's" designer

"Barracuda" of Tarrant

"Barracuda" — very long in the water!

generated in Hamble was back in 1970 when, on the 18th of October, Charles 'Chay' Blyth began his successful round the world circumnavigation in his 59 foot ketch, *British Steel*, to become the first person to complete a non stop solo westabout — that was for real.

Back in the fictional world of Howards Way, I tracked down the Barracuda's designer, Tony Castro, in his quaint thatched cottage in Satchell Lane, Hamble. He came to Britain in 1983, and has been designing boats for eleven years, following a job as a Naval Architect. I asked him what he thought of the way his brainchild was portrayed on the screen.

"Quite nice, I didn't feel any objections", he said. "Personally, I thought that it was a shame that a lot of the best footage wasn't used. There was a particular day that we went out into the open sea, and were filmed from a helicopter. It must have looked amazing. The helicopter was just 20 metres away, and we were all suffering from the downwash.

I think that within the profession we all tend to look at the scenes much more critically, and we're therefore the hardest to satisfy. But the producer's job is to make it appealing to people who know nothing about boats, and the audience ratings show that he has indeed succeeded. If we'd had our way, there would have been a lot more boat and sailing scenes. But probably at the expense of a lot of viewers."

The *Barracuda of Tarrant,* the boat used in the series and built at the Elephant boatyard, was used as a model from which the mould was taken, for the production models which are being made by Sadler Yachts. The deck of the initial boat is actually a GRP production deck. Often the plug is discarded. This is because the company involved is unwilling to spend such extra money as is required to turn this full-sized model into a completed boat. But in this case, because it was early days and no-one really knew if either Barracuda, or the series was going to be a success, the decision was taken to complete it. This was an attempt to recover the money invested in its design and initial

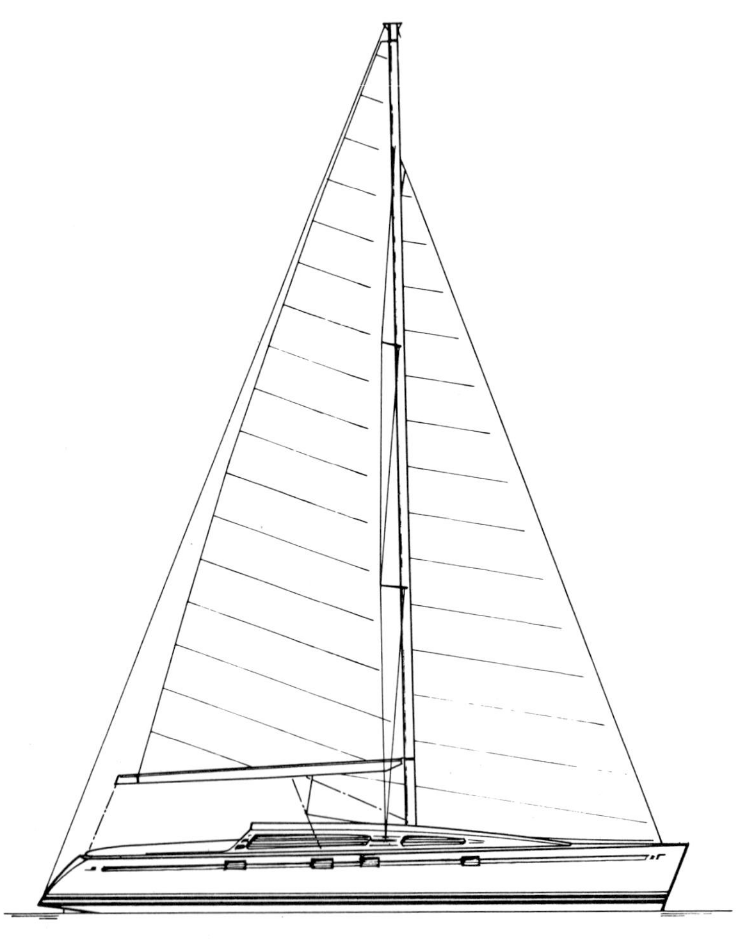

The modern design of the 45′ racing yacht — "Barracuda"

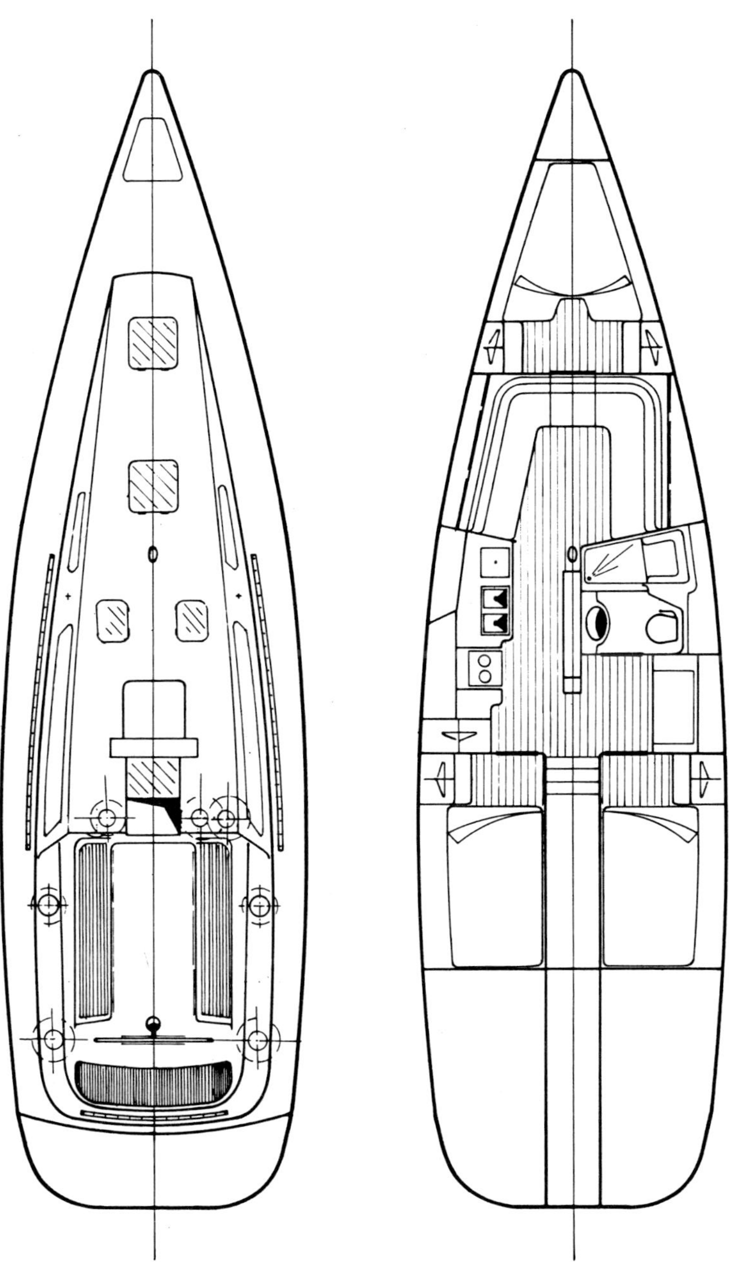

Layout of "Barracuda" above and below deck

construction by selling it to someone in case all else failed.

The Barracuda is, according to Tony, the first lightweight GRP cruising boat of its type put into production in Europe. It's 45' and has an unusually long waterline compared with its length. This enables it to use a large proportion of its length to produce speed. Additional features include the twin rudders. These increase the boat's directional stability. When a boat heels over with a central rudder, a large proportion of it comes out of the water rendering it ineffective. With a twin rudder, that's quite the opposite, because as the boat heels over, the other one really comes into its own, and digs further in.

In addition to these features, the boat has a lifting keel with a big bulb at the bottom to produce better stability. Draft is something that all the cruising people complain about, because they like to go to the beach and into small harbours. For this reason, the keel is designed to lift up and allow access to the shallow waters. Also, the sail plane has a fractional rig. The sail in the front is very much smaller than the sail at the back. The mast, as a result, is slightly further forward in the boat, creating positive characteristics in directional control, mostly off the wind when going very fast. Each of those three things blend produce what, in the yachting world, is considered to be an exciting design concept that works.

Following its construction, the boat was sold, chartered and hired to the BBC. It made a lot of money when the rights were sold to the Sadler company, and this covered Elephant boatyard's building bill.

I asked Tony how the *Barracuda of Tarrant* came to be featured in the television series.

"Bob Fisher and I were about 300 miles out from Hong Kong in a race called the China Sea Race. As you can imagine, it was quite a long race, and we had a lot of time to talk about a lot of things. I remember one night it was blowing quite hard and yet the boat was not going particularly fast. We were thinking, 'Gee, with all this wind, wouldn't it be nice if we had something that was really

Tony Castro's and Bob Fisher's ideal kind of boat — "Barracuda"

"Barracuda" — on her way to another race

exhilarating and exciting?'. So for the next three nights we designed our ideal kind of boat. That was it, we thought no more about it. Then some time later, Bob turned up and said, 'Do you remember the boat we were talking about? Well, what do you think about incorporating the idea into a programme that a friend of mine's putting together?' The programme was the story of a boatyard, and somewhere along the line the boatyard story was adapted to incorporate this revolutionary boat, which at least when we started was a pretty far fetched thing to build in Europe. There were similar boats in the Pacific, but in Europe there wasn't anything like it. Before I knew it, I was designing this dream boat, and top of all that, having a TV series written around it."

With such a wealth of experience in the technical aspects of yachting, I thought that Tony would be the ideal person to offer advice to the BBC...

"I helped out while Bob Fisher was away in Australia doing the 12 metres", he explained. "Mainly just answering a few questions which revolved around some chats with the scriptwriters and the set designers. They came to my home office here in Hamble and saw how it worked. They took some photographs for reference in an attempt to make the new scripts even more authentic. As the overall storyline develops, I've tried to do my best to help the BBC come up with a solution to the Lynnette drama which is realistic and doesn't upset anybody, but what they will eventually choose, I don't know. I think that they underestimated the reaction from the sailing industry to the catamaran accident scenes. Everyday you see car smashes on TV, but no one calls up the BBC every second minute complaining about it. But because Howards' Way is such a new thing, it has created a lot of repercussions. I think that the line of direction followed by the 'powers that be' is that the way to generate the number of viewers, and ultimately the success of the series, is to play fairly heavily on the disaster element. Unfortunately, I think that this is part of the British 1980's general problem, which

"Barracuda" — on her mooring at Lymington

Tony Castro — more designs on the way

is that success is a really bad word in this country. In contrast, everything you see in America is about success."

He gave me a sideways glance, leaned back in his chair, and with a knowing smile told me that, in the future the series will PROBABLY(!) provide a better blend of the two.

If you really fancy buying up a piece of Howards' Way, then the Barracuda 45 is going into production with Sadler Yachts, with a price tag, at the time of writing, of £75,000, plus vat.

Although unspoken, it seems apparent that Tony has been the inspiration of the Tom Howard character in the series, but are his ideals the same?

"In the real world, you can't just say 'wood is better than plastic', or vice versa. They've both got their own merits. However, the plastic production Barracuda has beaten the original wooden one.

Wooden boats are very expensive to build because of the labour. If anybody thinks that a yard like Mermaid is cheap then they're kidding themselves, and so when it comes to production boats, then GRP is usually the only way to make a project financially viable.

In modern boats we often use a mixture of wood with glass sheeted over the top. Usually though, people tend to go for one thing or the other, mainly by the availability of the person to do it. And that's a fact that is often overlooked when the virtues of either form of construction is superficially assessed."

The grin returned to Tony's face when I began quizzing him about anything for the new series of Howards' Way. It appears that the BBC have sworn him to secrecy. However, he did admit that he was working on some 'secret projects', so perhaps we can expect some new boats in the series soon.

In the first series, we saw model boats in a water tank being used to assist in the design of the Barracuda. In real life this technique is very rarely used, because the designer knows what characteristics the boat should have, and so the expense of scale models isn't required. However, it's perfectly plausible, especially for Barracuda, as it is useful to check some characteristics. And it certainly made some nice footage.

When the production began on the first series, it had a very low budget. Apparently this is improving, but a lot of people, including Tony Castro, were getting involved voluntarily. In fact, according to Tony, Howards' Way's total budget for a whole series is roughly equal to a single episode of Dallas. This must make the director's job extremely difficult, and although we can all criticise, they have, in the circumstances, done extremely well. But why choose the Hamble River as the base for the filming?

"Bob Fisher and I realised that the whole concept was here on our doorsteps. I mean, with Rolfe's place and the Elephant we have the typical place, so much that it's not true. It's just so close." Perhaps Tom Richardson really IS Jack Rolfe!

The Lynnette Catamaran

From the success of the Barracuda, and it's stylish portrayal on the screen, we turn to the dismal end that befell the infamous 'Lynnette' catamaran. She sunk amidst speculation of a design fault at the end of the second series. Ian King, from Lymington, who co-designed and built the boat in conjunction with his partner David Allan-Williams in his back garden, was understandably unhappy with the portrayal of the craft. I asked him whether the BBC had, at the outset, told him how the catamaran was to be written into the scripts. . .

"The information that we were given changed throughout, and we found ourselves being drawn into an area which we didn't really consider to be in the best interests of our business". he said. "After agreeing to let the BBC use the boat, we were told that they were going to paint a fake crack onto the beam, but it would be taken back to the yard and repaired and that would be that. The next thing we knew was when some of the props people phoned us up and started asking for parts of bow sections and so on. We

"The Lynette" or "Alien"

thought 'Oh! Oh!' and eventually found out that the boat was destined for a sinking. As soon as we found this out, we informed the BBC that we would be withdrawing the catamaran from use. The BBC panicked, initially from the blow to the scripts, and also from the press that we were getting about the scene, both locally and nationally. It was about that time that we found out that someone was going to be killed in the scene, and that was the last straw. Things got very nasty for a week or so with the BBC, but then they started phoning up and requesting advice on technical aspects."

The whole script for the third series relies upon the outcome of the sinking and, at the end of the second series, we were left wondering if the Mermaid yard was doomed and, if Tom Howard would, as designer, be held responsible.

Ian King, co-designer and builder of "The Lynette"/"Alien"

Inside Ian King's factory (Green Marine) where a 50′ boat for the Admirals Cup Trials is being built for Ernest Juer

The yard as viewed from outside

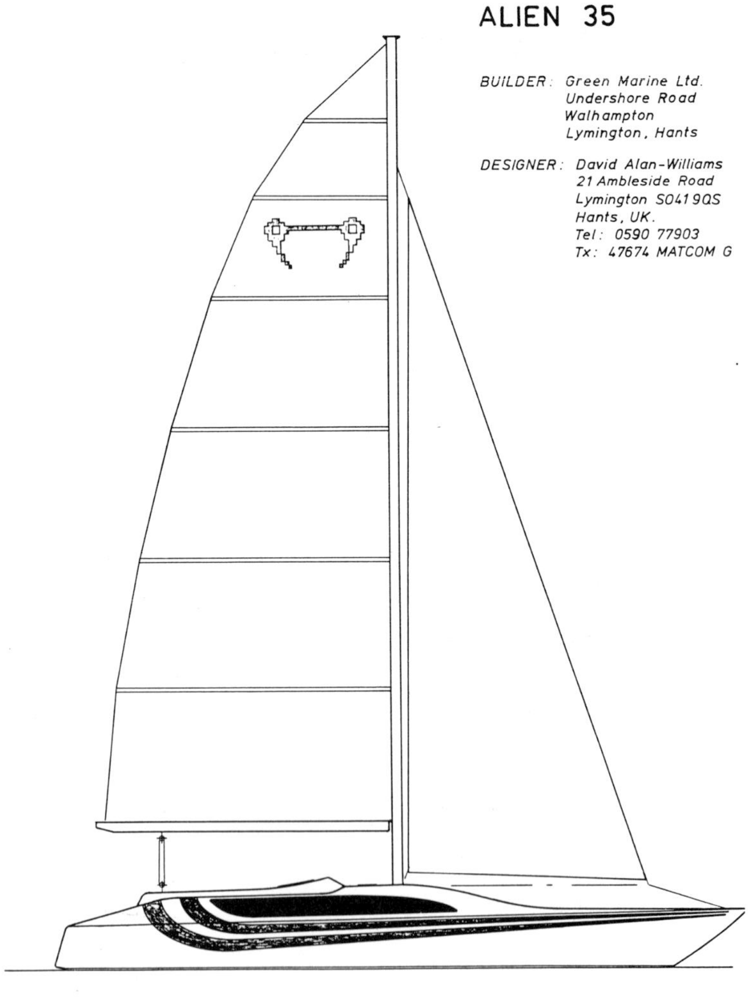

The futuristic design of "Alien" ("Lynette") was ideal for the series

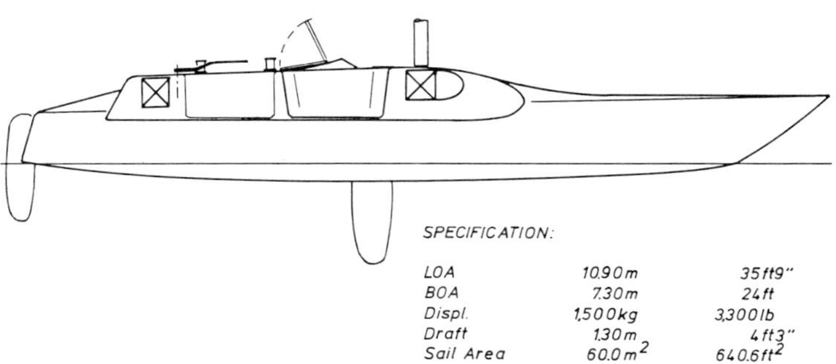

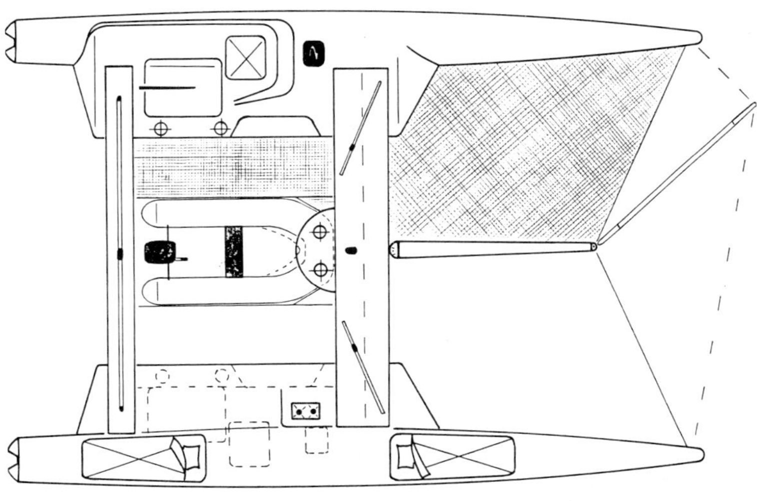

Layout of "Alien"

Lymington Marina

I wondered if Ian King had been consulted about the outcome of the sinking.

"We were asked, and have provided several options", he said. "We've tried to think of something that won't adversly effect either our suppliers, or ourselves as designers and builders. As far as we're concerned, this rules out the possibility of faulty resins, and the possibility of a design problem. Perhaps the most plausible solution would be for the boat to strike a semi-submerged object in the water."

Luckily, Ian King's customer's don't seem to confuse fact with fiction too easily, and so once the word got around about what was to happen to the boat, everyone seemed to accept it as the story that it was. But I did hear a lot of people expressing opinions that what the BBC did was wrong, but that's showbusiness I guess. If you fancy a catamaran, then you can buy the Lynnette, which is in real life called an 'Alien', depending on internal fittings, for around £40,000 to £50,000. Making the 'knock down' sale price of £38,000 in the series quite realistic.

"Alien" on her mooring at Lymington

"Alien"

I spotted the catamaran, minus it's 'Lynnette' stickers, moored in Lymington, where some of the filming took place. I wonder if David or Ian could have foreseen the nation holding their breath over the portrayal of the boat, that they built over a period of two months in Ian's back garden, back in 1982, after being made redundant from their previous boatbuilding jobs?

I asked Ian how the BBC came to approach him with a view to using his catamaran.

"Bob Fisher, who was acting as the series technical adviser, was looking around for a hi-tech, modern looking multihull for the series. He saw ours, and asked if he could use it. We thought, unfortunately, that being involved in such a major national series was very likely to do us some good, especially after hearing how the Barracuda had benefited from the exposure.

The BBC persuaded us to paint it, get it ready very quickly, and deliver it for its first filming session. Unfortunately, even with the rushing around, the BBC weren't ready for filming, and we had to hang about for hours waiting."

At first glance, Lymington appears to be an ideal location for 'Tarrant', with its cobbled streets and pretty harbour. It seems to have everything going for it photographically, except for a suitable boatyard around which to base the series. In talking to the yachting fraternity, it seems that Bursledon's Elephant yard is indeed unique, being small, picturesque and family run. In the Lymington area, the work largely revolves around mooring and general maintenance.

Prior to the fictional accident, the catamaran was depicted as a great boat, and it would be hard to dispute the effectiveness of the sailing scenes. Did Ian agree?

"Bob Fisher dressed up in Tom Howard's clothes provided some convincing footage, as no one else seemed to know much about sailing. There was one time when, although the shot had to depict a solo sail, we had about eight people on the boat, all hiding below out of sight. These included cameramen, sound men, Bob Fisher, and the actors. This made the boat run in a slightly unusual fashion, and slowed it down quite a bit. However, having said that, there was one shot where we had to sail across the Solent, and we travelled so fast that the cameras weren't even ready!"

With payment from the BBC of £200 per day for the use of the boat, which is the highest rate that anyone I've spoken to has ADMITTED to receiving, Ian can't really feel too hard done by.

"Most of the BBC are nice helpful people," he said. "I suppose we've all got to make our money somehow."

So, as the story unfolds and it becomes clear that the design was not at fault, will the catamaran be promoted as the Lynnette, or keep under it's own name of 'Alien'?

"I wouldn't dream of calling our boat the Lynnette, it sound to me like some kind of sanitary towel. No, we'll DEFINITELY revert to its real name."

The Flying Fish

The final boat in the trio most often featured in the series was the 'Flying Fish'. This was shown as being owned by Tom

A "Laser 28" — in the series as "The Flying Fish"

Howard, who sold it for £20,000 and used the money, together with his redundancy payment from the aircraft factory, to buy into the Mermaid Yard. Avril Rolfe was the secret purchaser, but eventually she sold it once more to buy back her father's shares which had been sold to pay off his gambling debts. Did you follow all that?

David Hopkins, the sales negotiator with 'Laser' at Port Hamble explains how he was first approached, with a view to using the 'Laser 28, *Flying Fish* for the series:

"Bob Fisher (again), was looking for a fast hi-tech modern boat that would fit the image of a brilliant young designer, (Tom Howard), from an aircraft factory. The *Flying Fish* apparently fitted the bill as a modern high performance boat."

The Laser 28 would cost around £25,000 to buy. The one chosen for the filming was a demonstrator boat that had already been christened the *Flying Fish*. Recently, it has been sold to a buyer on the Isle of Wight, so it seems unlikely that it will feature further in the series. We've heard about how Tony and Ian felt about their boats portrayal, and so what does David think of the *Flying Fish's* on screen exploits?

"The sailing scenes could perhaps have been more exciting, if the boat had been sailed by experts, rather than film crews and actors. In a big breeze it could have looked superb. Bob Fisher was on board giving advice, but the sort of boat that it is, unless you've got a team of six professionals, you can't show it to its best advantage. From my own point of view, I would have like to have seen that, but I suppose that would have been too expensive, as each young crew-member would want a daily rate of at least £50 to do something like that."

Bob Fisher actually had the boat in 1985, and was campaigning and racing it during that year. This combined with his job with the BBC seems to have resulted in the boat 'drifting' into the series. The BBC had access to the boat for about 12 months, but the filming was all done in separate sections. This was easy to arrange because it was a demonstrator boat. Most people unfortunately don't realise that it's

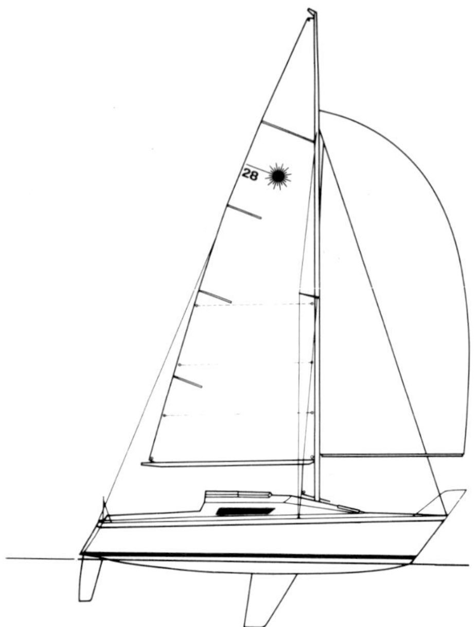

"Laser 28" — the hi-tech modern boat

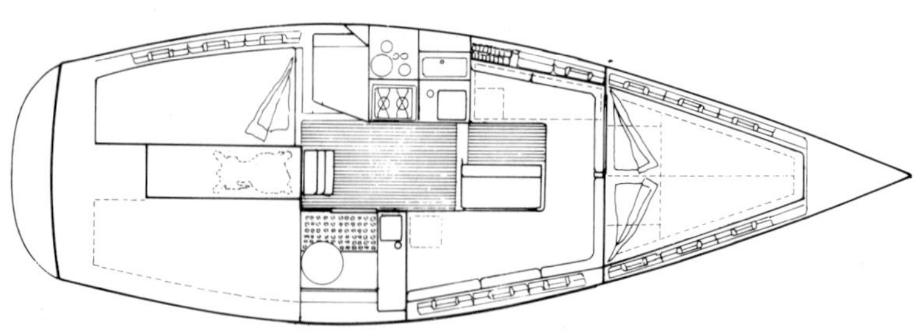

The surprisingly roomy layout of "The Flying Fish"

a Laser 28 in the series, and so I asked if the exposure did result in a positive effect on sales.

"It didn't actually do anything for boosting sales," explained David, "However, it did create a lot of interest when it was first shown at Earls Court in 1986.

The people who wanted to go for a sail on it seemed to be interested mainly because it was the Flying Fish from the series, as opposed to serious purchasing enquiries. If you can't pick out the time wasters, then that's a minus point."

Everyone that we've heard from so far seems to extol the virtues of wooden boats to an extent. I wondered if David's views co-incided, or not.

"There's for and against both really. Wooden boats need a lot more maintenance, but nowadays, with the advent of epoxy systems, cold moulded wooden boats can be virtually maintenance free, and there's nothing nicer to look at than a wooden boat. But to build boats in vast numbers, fibreglass is the only way to go."

"I thought that the rivalry between Jack Rolfe, and Tom

David Hopkins — in the Laser factory

The large press used in construction of the boats

Howard was very good. I don't think it was overplayed, because there are people around, just like Jack Rolfe, in little yards all around the country. I don't really sympathise with them, but they're doing all right simply because people still want wooden boats, although not so many now. The trouble is, if they wanted to build a production run of wooden boats, then it would cost a lot of money, and frankly, the skills aren't around to build them nowadays. There used to be lots of apprentices leaving yards who were qualified on wooden boats. When I served my apprenticeship, every yard had about 25 to 50 people doing five year apprenticeships. Now, they have one or two here and there. These days you just can't afford to have somebody chipping away at a piece of wood, day in day out, when you can make a mould and churn out thousands of boats."

I hope that Tom Richardson of the Elephant Yard, or, for that matter, Jack Rolfe of the Mermaid, doesn't hear him say that!

There are, as we have heard, mixed feelings throughout

The strengthening structure ready for installation

"Laser 28" ready for interior fittings

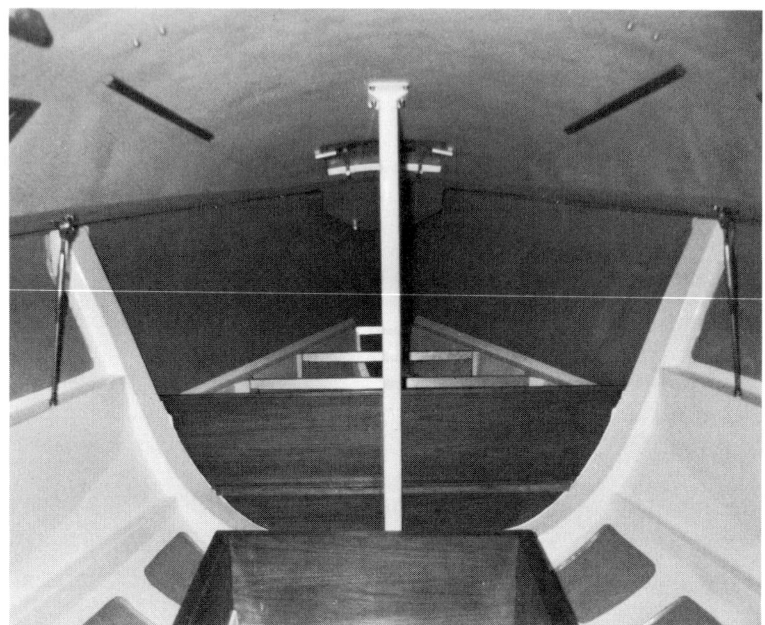

The interior of a "Laser 28" prior to fitting out

The "Laser 28" moored at Port Hamble

the yachting world about the artistic value, or otherwise, of the Lynnette portrayal. David feels that the whole thing was 'bad news' for the expanding multihull market, and does sympathise with Ian King. He explains. . .

"We were well aware of what the Flying Fish was going to be used for and made quite clear how it was going to be portrayed. We know it was going to be the fastest thing ever seen, and it was going to be a wonderful race winning boat. I felt sorry for the catamaran people because they didn't know what was coming. That sort of thing on the TV is bad for the image of the catamaran. Now, millions of viewers who know nothing about sailing are left with the impression that a multihull is dangerous. Everything can break, all boats have got their weak points, whether it be cats or monohulls, but I don't think its fair to criticise any particular type of boat.

Apparently it appears that there were grumbles from some of the locals in respect of the series. They felt, completely wrongly as far as I'm concerned, that they were

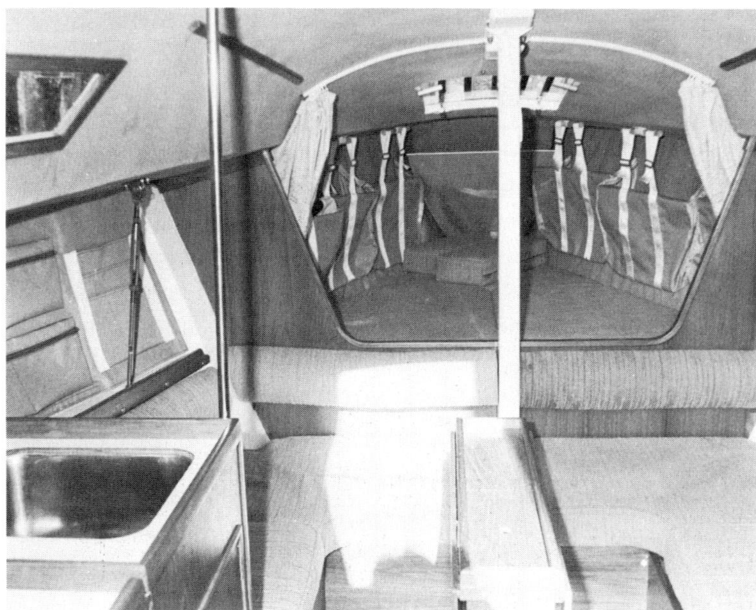

The comfortable interior of "The Flying Fish"

The "Laser 28" — ready for work

themselves being branded as 'Ken Masters', or 'Jack Rolfes', and got a bit upset about it. David holds with my view as well and believes that the series has done nothing but good, because now everybody wants to see the area, and, above all, it's depicted the river as being a nice place. Another spin-off is the fact that property prices in the area are rocketing. But surely David was sick of people snooping around Port Hamble with cameras. . .

"When the boat's been moored out here, lots of people have come down and wanted to have a look, and we're quite happy to show them round the boat. We've also taken complete novices out sailing, during the regatta. It was great fun and we used the Flying Fish as a boost, it sold raffle tickets and made money for the Inshore Lifeboat."

When I enquired whether, with hindsight, he would, had he been given the opportunity, have changed anything in the series, it was back to the Lynnette again;

"I don't like the way that there are disasters happening left right and centre. I mean, there's always seems to be something going wrong in the sailing world like sinking catamarans, boats blowing up, boats cracking and so forth. It leaves people with the impression that sailing is a hazardous occupation. I am sure they could have created excitement in other ways without worrying people. I think that they could have included some more sailing scenes out on the water."

Most of the locals that are moaning about the likening of characters on screen to themselves are probably getting worried, but I just couldn't get any names to follow up. . .

"Oh yes, they're all around here actually," said David with a grin. "But I wouldn't like to say who they were. The Jack Rolfes definitely exist, but I must admit, I've yet to meet a Ken Masters type."

So finally, did Laser get any financial reward from the series?

"Nothing! But the last time they used the boat, we did charge them, as they wanted it delivered to Lymington. We got a delivery crew to do it. They charged us, so we charged the BBC. I do think that it's a bit unfortunate that no-one realised it was a Laser 28. They didn't zoom in on the sail or the sign on the sail. In contrast, everybody knows the Barracuda."

Pubs of the Series

The Jolly Sailor

It's clear who pulls the punches in the series, but who pulls the pints? Bursledon certainly has its own fair share of quaint pleasant hostelries. But the one that features most regularly in the filming is the Jolly Sailor. Like the Elephant Boatyard, it is situated in Lands End Road, and is reached by a steep footpath winding down from the road above the pub's roof level, to the riverside entrance. This is the only possible land approach. However, for yachtsmen, there is an alternative. A specially constructed jetty reaches out from the pub into the river. In summer, it's often full of customers sitting at the little wooden tables enjoying their food and drink. This jetty offers the river folk the opportunity to moor their tenders, and gain direct access to the pub. Even the most short-sighted sailor couldn't fail to spot the huge sign proclaiming the name of the pub in big black letters against a white background.

The Jolly Sailor was originally a flat fronted house with sash windows. The present bows are a fairly recent addition. Until it was sold and modernised, it was a simple little waterfront meeting place where, on winter evenings, perhaps a dozen or so locals congregated, and at closing time had to negotiate the steep path up to the road above roof level, whilst 'under the influence'.

The pub exists exactly as it is portrayed on the screen. I

A clue to where it's hidden

The Jolly Sailor from the water

The picturesque interior of the Jolly Sailor

Jack Mellan — landlord for eight years

asked the landlord, Jack Mellan, how long the BBC were filming there for...

"They've been using us over the last two years. They had a complete schedule for all of the sequences, coming and going between here and the boatyard for blocks of between three and five days. Normally in March or April time, and again in August."

I guessed that it must have been difficult to remain open for business.

"No, they were really very good. Being a busy place, we did insist that they were out of the way prior to opening. They would get down here at about seven in the morning and set up, beginning at around 7.30 and finished by about eleven. Sometimes they over-run, but on the whole they were very good. They also came down one Sunday evening. They had a very late evening scene, around about eleven o'clock. They were completely set up and were filming for about an hour before closing time, so there was a lot of people, a lot of interest and it was on a lovely warm summer evening too."

After eight years as landlord, Jack's decided to call it a day, feeling that it's time he regained his social freedom. With the Jolly Sailor, it's nothing to be required to work for about seventy-four hours a week, increasing in peak periods to ninety six or more. Apparently the series has made a slight impact on trade, but this tends to chase off the business customers, who are looking for a quiet lunchtime meeting place.

Originally it is believed that the pub was a house, and possibly in the 1800's, a grain store. The grain ships used to anchor off and unload. In fact, according to Jack, there's an old tunnel outside and a pony and trap used to carve it's way through and come out by the station, cross a ford, load up on barges and continue onto Botley Mill.

I thought that the regulars would have been very excited about the prospect of their pub being used in a National television series, but it seems that I was wrong. Jack explains why...

"Quite frankly, they were indifferent to the whole thing. I

The Jolly's main bar — familiar to all viewers of the series

The cosy back bar of the Jolly Sailor

think there was a slight interest in the programme itself, in things like camera angles used, and suchlike. I always hear the comments of 'what a load of rubbish', but week after week everybody seems to be watching it, and it's being discussed across all of the social classes.

You can count on your fingers the number of real regulars you get in here. I don't know where the rest come from. Week after week, month after month, they're all different. Some come from the river, some from the colleges, you can almost set your calender by them. In January and February, the 'yachties' come in while they're down here working on their boats, having disappeared since October. People are travelling from all over the country to get to their boats, and so, when they arrive, the last place they want to be is in a pub, They want to get aboard and head for the Isle of Wight. Ironically, we get more people from the Isle of Wight, France and Holland over here than the locals sometimes."

Following Jack Mellan's departure, the pub is being taken over by a small brewery called Hall and Woodhouse who will clearly wish to advertise. Only time will tell if they will pursue the Howards' Way angle. However, most local people are united in hoping that whatever they do, they keep it subtle.

Contrary to popular belief, the majority of the bar scenes shown in the series weren't made in the Jolly Sailor at all, but on an identical studio set at the Pebble Mill studios in Birmingham. The likeness is uncannily accurate, and they even constructed the window through which a yachting panorama can be seen. I, for one, was convinced that the real bar had been used. However, before you get too disappointed, the back bar of the pub WAS featured. Due to the dim lighting, the BBC had to provide considerable additional illumination, and were faced with the problem of maintaining the unique cosy 'olde worlde' atmosphere. Jack tells me that they went out of their way to be unobtrusive, and believes that one of the main reasons that they built up the mock front bar was to avoid interfering with this trading schedules.

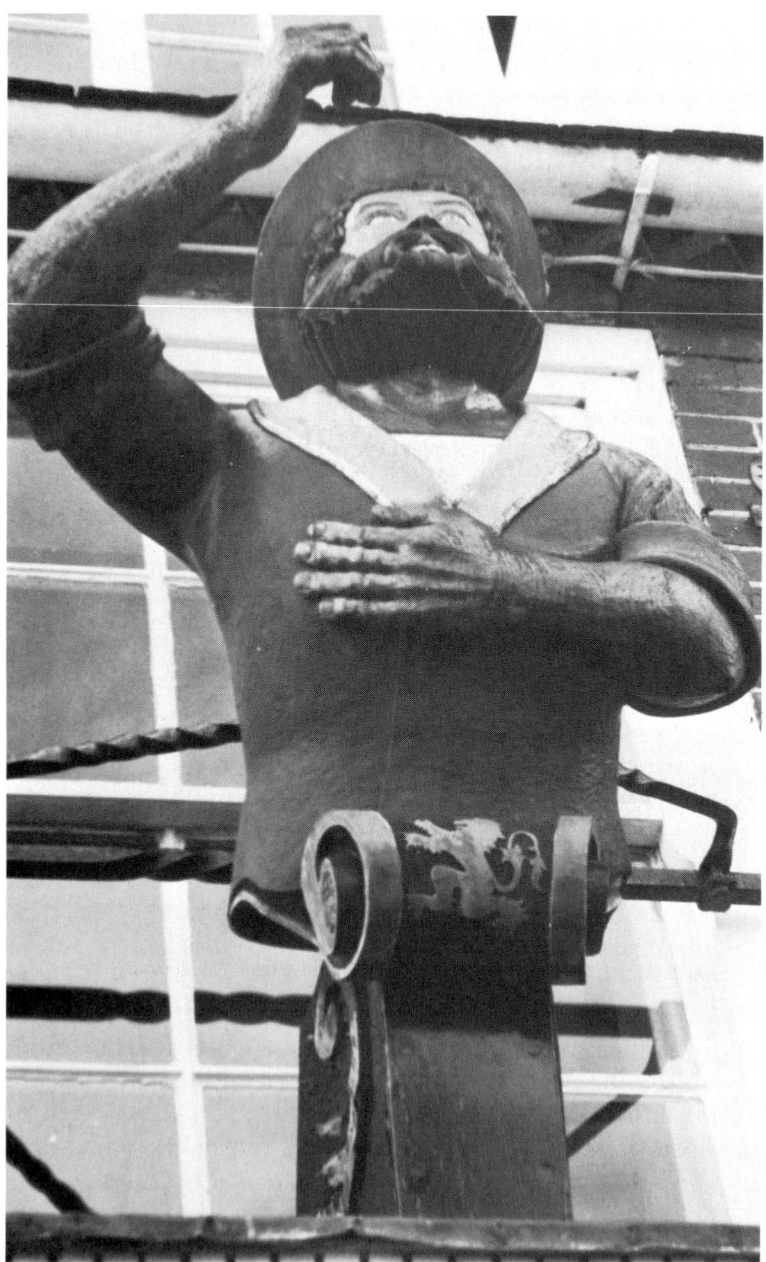

The figurehead above the main door

I asked him how the BBC approached him...

"They contacted us through one of their London offices, and asked if we would mind them using the pub. They told us that they had signed an agreement with the Elephant Boatyard to build a boat and do a series on the yard. We didn't realise that it was going to be as extensive as it was, imagining it to be some kind of documentary." he said.

Being an old pub in an affluent location, it seemed a fair bet that it had been a social venue for some famous people over the years. By all accounts, I was right!

"Prince Andrew's been in twice, visiting Cowes Week with his entourage of detectives. He just turned up unannounced. People did recognise him, but they were very kind and just left him to have a good evening, which is, I think as it should be. Also, Ted Heath, (the ex-Prime Minister) used to come down here when his yacht *Morning Cloud* was on the river. He's got some friends in the village. Also, the scriptwriters from the series have recently been in, so it looks like the Jolly's going to remain in the limelight for a while longer yet."

Jack isn't against the Southampton Tourist Board's plans to bring over 4000 visitors to the area, but points out, without remorse, that he hasn't got a car park suitable for coaches. (In fact he hasn't got one at all!) Although he was approached and asked if he would allow the large boats that are destined to carry the sightseers up the river to dock on his pontoon, — he declined. But why?

"A hundred people at a time were being brought up on boats of about 60 tons. If the guy gets the docking wrong, with that weight, even moving at one mile an hour, it would demolish my pontoon, so I said to him that it was best if they had a re-think on that. Also, they wanted to come up at about 6 in the evening which means that right from the minute we open, we'd have that, and all our other trade. It would have been a hell of a job coping."

It seems as if the pub is a fantastic meeting place, where exciting adventures are planned over a few pints.

Although not seen very often in the series, the rear of the pub is also very attractive

"Yes, the back bar is a great collecting spot for people who are going abroad on their boats. I really bought the pub to learn about deep water sailing," said Jack. "I've learnt everything from the characters that inhabit the back bar. As well as that, I bought a boat and sailed solo to the West Indies and back. I wouldn't have been able to do that without the help of a lot of these people. They're great.

I'm planning a trip up to Iceland to go through the Arctic Circle. And again, the crew are coming from the 'back bar regulars'. I enjoy adventures. I've even cycled across Australia from Perth to Sydney, sleeping in the bush. I need to do different things."

A few years ago there was a common link between the pubs in the area, in the shape of Don Taylor. He was once the local postman, but could clearly see that there was a lucrative potential market on his doorstep. He bought the Fox and Hounds and the Jolly Sailor at Bursledon, the Old Ship at Swanwick, and the White Harte in Hamble. All very unique pubs that really expanded. They were nothing until he took them over and transformed them.

I asked Jack whether he thought that the storyline of the series was believable:

"I think very much so. There are people about who have got money, want to get into things, and are prepared to take a chance. However, at times it's a bit far-fetched. I've no doubt that a lot of these things do go on around here on the quiet, and I've certainly seen some characters around here like Jack Rolfe and Tom Howard."

Was it worth it? With all the upheaval of film crews, directors, lighting and equipment, surely the BBC must have made it well worth Jack's while.

"We made £50 per session. If they came in the morning they paid £50, and if they came again in the afternoon it was another £50. It didn't matter to me, the money's not important. They really do work. I've even seen them up at the boatyard at midnight. There doesn't seem to be any upsets or 'hanky pankys', they just get on with it."

The front of the Jolly — up close

The Lone Barn

Several other local pubs made fleeting appearances in the series, some for no more than a couple of minutes. However, the upheaval and attention to detail by the film crews often resulted in dozens of people being involved, sometimes for a complete day, to finish a single short scene. One such pub is the Fox and Hounds, and adjoining Lone Barn at Hungerford Bottom.

They filmed two sections at the pub. One at the front of the Fox and Hounds which took about two hours, and one in the Lone Barn that lasted virtually all day. For the barn, they set up at nine o'clock in the morning and spent the whole day working. This resulted in just one and a half minutes on the screen. There were forty people involved all the time. I asked the Landlord, Terry McEvoy if it affected opening times.

"No, we were expecting them, and so we traded in the Fox and Hounds bar instead of the Barn. They did say that they would be finished in time for the Barn to open in the

The Lone Barn and Fox and Hounds

The alcove in the Lone Barn

Lone Barn interior — featuring the various old implements

evening, but in the end they didn't complete until about half past eight. It was good fun though. We had a lot of customers in, keeping unusually quiet and poking their noses through the door to watch what was going on."

The BBC used the car park as a base for their equipment, as it was handy for the Bondfield (Howards') House location up the road in Kew Lane. All the equipment was kept ready, and sent up when required via 'walkie-talkie' contact. When they filmed in the Lone Barn, you wouldn't have recognised it unless you knew it, because all you saw was a little alcove.

The chef was involved in the filming. He is in the scene where they carve the meat when Tom and Avril are in the barn having a meal. Also, in the first series when they were filmed outside the Fox and Hounds, Terry's wife was collecting glasses and his grandson and daughter were sat with some of the locals on the end of a table, as Jack Rolfe staggered by.

Again, the BBC's attention to detail was evident in the filming at the Lone Barn. They blocked all of the windows up to simulate night-time, moved the great big wooden centre table and ran a railway for their camera to track on. Also, they took some of the old artefacts off of the walls because they felt that it looked too cluttered, preferring to direct their viewers' attention to the characters, as opposed to the background.

It seems that the decision to film at the pub was a spur of the moment thing, as Terry explains;

"They were filming down the road in the garden at 'Hunt's Folly', and used to come up to the Fox and Hounds for a lunchtime snack and a drink. On noticing our large car park, they asked us if they could use it. In return, we were offered a shot of the pub in the finished series. Later, my wife enquired into the possibility of them staging a scene in the Lone Barn. To our surprise, they agreed."

Not to be outdone, the Fox and Hounds has, like the Jolly Sailor, had it's fair share of celebrity patrons over the years. These have included the character 'Adam Chance' from the 'Crossroads' series, Fern Britten, the TVS 'Coast to Coast' presenter, and John Noakes, of 'Blue Peter', 'get down Shep' fame. Apparently, he used to come in for a quiet drink every Monday night when he was living in the area.

With their abundance of car parking facilities and large bar area, the pub could easily have housed the Howards' Way weekend visitors, arranged by the Southampton Tourist Board. But alas, for Terry, the extra trade hasn't materialised. . .

"I was hoping that the coaches might do a tour round Bursledon, and visit the pub," he sighed. "Trouble is, the neighbouring residents won't put up with it. I'm always getting hassle with the traffic as it is!"

Several stars from the series visited the pub for a drink and a meal during the filming. I wondered if, after seeing them 'in the flesh' so to speak, Terry had any favourites.

"I like Lynne Howard, the blonde one, and my wife thinks that Freyer is terrific! I thoroughly enjoyed the series. Mind you, the reason I watch it is because it is local. It's nice to see local places. But I did see some things that I thought were

Lone Barn interior — this shows the table which had to be removed

wrong. When they were filming on Bursledon bridge, they were going over it one way in a car, and the next thing you know, the car's going the other way, but I guess that's just television's poetic licence. I thought that the storyline was good. I liken Freyer to JR in Dallas, which is another of my favourite series."

Again and again, despite being on a relatively limited budget, the BBC crew's attention to detail prevails over all else. Just listen to this. . .

"Our chef wears a hat that has a hole in the top and they took about an hour and a half to get his hat right. They had to put different coloured paper in the top because the lights were shining down and causing problems with the colour balances in the camera. Their attention to detail for just a little tiny thing like that was amazing.

They left us a curtain rail that they put up in several of the alcoves that looks very nice. They did it in three alcoves, because they had extras sitting in there pretending to eat a meal. It fascinated me watching them film here. They did about six dummy runs without filming. But when they actually did the real thing, it was all over and done with in a very short time, and it seemed to me that for all the time they were here, and all the hassle that they went through, it was really not worthwhile. I expected the finished scene, after all that, to last a lot longer than the minute or so we saw.

My chef took about five days to prepare the food. It was fantastic. There were two salmon leaping on a gilt plate, some briskets of beef with lobsters on the side, and little houses made out of bread with 'Weetabix' roofs. It looked absolutely lovely. The table was set magnificently too, and I thought 'they're going to have to feature that', but all they did was pan by it, showing it for no more than four seconds. They did pay us for the food though. In fact, the customers did very well because the BBC didn't want it after they had finished, and we were selling a lobster salad for three pounds. A whole lobster with a salad! I would have thought that they could buy plastic things. But I enjoyed it, they can come back here filming as many times as they like."

Terry McEvoy (landlord) and his wife

Terry makes a very interesting point here;

"I don't see why they called the village Tarrant. They talk about Southampton, Petersfield and other towns, but they don't call the village Bursledon. They were put to unnecessary trouble changing the station signs and things, it's daft."

If you're wondering how much money Terry made from the filming, then it can be told. It was a mere £25, which he thoughtfully gave to charity. It isn't ITV, you know!

Hamble — The Italian Job

The Hamble River, the stretch of water that cuts a swathe through the Hampshire countryside on its way out into the Solent, has, for a great many years, been a mecca for yachtsmen far and wide. In fact, during the warm summer months, the boats almost outnumber the cars.

There can be few villages in Britain that can boast, over the centuries, to have had a priory, a Norman church, a castle, and to have played a significant role in the country's aviation and maritime history. In 1418, the biggest ship ever built in England at that time was brought to Hamble for fitting out, the *Grace Dieu*. During the following centuries, most of the village's activities continued to be maritime based. Up until the beginning of the 20th century, the population of Hamble had averaged around 200-300 people, but with the development of the aviation industry in the village, the population increased dramatically to about 3000.

During the First World War, the first Englishman to fly, A.V. Roe, came to the village and built a large aircraft factory, as did another company, Fairey Aviation. Through these, many famous aviation people have been connected with Hamble, including Bert Hinkler, Amy Johnston, and Juan De Cierva, the designer of the first autogyro. And now, the brilliant young aircraft designer turned boatbuilder, Tom Howard.

The Royal Southern Yacht Club's premises have been converted from a row of cottages built in 1818. And Portland

The High Street of Hamble

Compass Point Chandlery — an Italian delicatessen?

House, which featured in the Italian Honeymoon scene, is believed to have been built as far back as 1550. Above the door there is an insurance plaque that indicates that the householder has insured his property against fire. This was to show the private company's brigade which houses it could attend to in the event of a blaze (in the days before the fire service was available to all).

Before the Second World War, most of the foreshore next to the quay was mud and marsh, right up to the road, with a number of hards giving access to the river. During the war years, the American forces reclaimed this land, and used it to repair their patrol and landing craft.

The village and its surroundings played an important part in the series which has, according to the Hamble to Warsash ferryman, Ray Sedgwick, had a pleasingly positive effect on local business.

"Lots more people want to explore the place now, and it's boosted the weekend trade considerably throughout the year. Probably because, at the moment, it's still a new thing. People want to know where everything was filmed, how long it took, and so on. The snag is that it's all so different now from when they were filming. Everything was decorated then, and the BBC brought quite a lot of scenery in especially for the programme. In some cases, I had a job to recognise it myself."

It's rumoured that there's been a ferry at Hamble since 1493, proving that there has always been a need to cross the river, as long as people lived nearby and, by all accounts, there's always been someone there to take them across. It's pleasant to see Ray Sedgwick placing more importance on the type of life he leads, than on earning a great deal of money. After an apprenticeship to become a skilled tool-maker, he chose to live a life of getting up at 4.45 each morning, and running a ferry in all weathers each day except Christmas and Boxing Day. In many villages, community life is dying, but at Hamble's ferry hard, Ray has created a friendly atmosphere.

The BBC only used Hamble for a short period, but

Ray Sedgewick — the ferry man

pressed several locations into service, including Mere House, (off of Hamble Green) for the garden party in the first series. Warsash village, across the river, was also used, and the 'Victoria Rampart' companies offices were featured as Ken Master's chandlery and Jan Howard's boutique.

Surprisingly, all the filming equipment was moved by road instead of the more direct river crossing. In the early days of the filming, all they had was an old single decker bus which acted as their canteen. But as time went on, and the series success was assured, more elaborate comforts began to arrive, and big BBC vans were used. They were often seen parked up on the hard, and at Hamble social club, next door to the service station that Leo was shown working in.

Warsash, across the river, was transformed into New York Harbour for the scene where Lynne successfully completed her solo crossing of the Atlantic in the Mermaid yard's brand new Barracuda yacht. Ray explains how they 'pulled it off' so convincingly. . .

"They changed the signs, and put up some American flags

Mere House overlooking the Hamble River

on the pontoon. They had a tug from the US base up at Marchwood, and that was it. If you take notice of what goes on around, then you could still spot all of the local stuff anyway, particularly the sailing college boats down the middle of the river. But most of the people that I have spoken to were absolutely amazed that it was done here."

What about Ken Master's chandlery?

"The Victoria Rampart offices, which were used, were untouched internally. They used the end of the office block. It had 'Master's Chandlery' written above it, and they decorated it with a few flags, a pair of oars, and an inflatable dingy. It was all done in a day, with the internal shots being filmed on a studio set," explained Ray.

The BBC's most ambitious scheme was to attempt to change a section of Hamble village into hot, sunny Italy, for the honeymoon scenes between Lynne and Claude. Impossible? No, they managed to make it very believable, and I for one didn't even recognise it. Straw and sand were put

The service station owned by Ken Masters, where Leo Howard worked

Victoria Rampart's office — Ken Master's chandlery

on the road, the Compass Point chandlery was turned into a delicatessen, and nearby Portland House had shutters put up to make it look more authentic. As with much of the film sequences, the finished shots were so brief, that I find it hard to justify all of the effort. It made about ten seconds on the screen, for a whole morning's work. But I suppose it's cheaper than sending the cast and crew to Italy, (though it can't be as much fun).

A lot of filming took place in Hamble, in conjunction with Claude Dupont's water skiing accident, that wasn't used. You may remember that he was run over by a boat whilst out on the water. It's thought that some of the footage was a bit too gruesome. Colin Olden, the cox of the Inshore Rescue, was out there watching them waste half a day's filming on elaborate scenes which were never shown.

I asked Ray whether he would have preferred it if the whole series had been shot elsewhere.

"No, I think that it's very good indeed for trade as far as I'm concerned. And actually, I think that a lot more could

The Compass Point — famous more for chandlery than Italian pastries

have been done around here to further encourage tourism. It seems that a lot of the local people, when they're asked about it, just don't want to know. Some of them are very offhand, particularly up at Bursledon.

Blue Star boats are committed by the Parish Council to run a trip boat, but they haven't put themselves out in any way yet, and have made all sorts of excuses. But, all things considered. I think that they could have done alright out of it. I'm sure that some better arrangement could have been made to accommodate interested people. Over in Southampton, they've got it organised, and if the Blue Funnel cruise people can fill their big trip boats up, then I'm jolly sure that we could pack out our little ones too. They plan to run a boat up here as far as the Jolly Sailor two or three times a week, carrying up to two hundred and fifty people, so there must be the demand."

After a seven days a week life on the river, Ray seemed to be the ideal person to ask who he thought the Ken Masters and Tom Howard characters were based upon?

"There's lots of likely candidates for that pair. In Tom's case, certainly, when you look at the yacht agencies. These youngsters think they know all the answers, but don't know the questions. They might be good on paper, but as far as practical experience goes, a lot of them know nothing at all.

You see loads of Ken Masters types in Hamble villages. They come and go, saying they're going to alter everything, and next thing, they've disappeared, quite often with other people's money. There's been a lot of that going on up in the village."

Ray also provided some straight sensible answers to the wood versus plastic boats argument.

"I think that if people want to use and enjoy a boat then they need a fibreglass one. In the old days, half the fun of owning a boat was to work on it. But people just haven't got the time nowadays. Way back, every boat was different, with the exception of the one-off racers, and that was the nice thing about it.

Just recently there have been a couple of GRP boats stolen

Ray Sedgewick with the author

The Royal Southern Yacht Club

from Moody's yard, on the Hamble. And it's very difficult to trace them quickly, because they all look the same. It's quite easy to change the name, and it could be a long time before anyone finds out that it's not the boat that it's supposed to be. In Moody's range alone, there must be hundreds on the river, and you can't tell one from another. They're all painted the same colour to start with, they've all got the same coloured dodgers on them and identical markings, with the exception of the name.

Most yards are geared up totally for plastic boats, and haven't got the facilities for coping with old timber ones. They all used to have slipways to pull them out of the water, which was kind and gentle to the boats, but now they use hoists instead, with the straps that go around underneath. This causes a lot of strain concentrated in one area. Timber boats, especially old ones, don't like to be lifted around like the modern ones."

When Chay Blyth came home from his round the world solo voyage in 1971, there were literally thousands of people lining the river. He actually left and returned to the Royal Southern Yacht Club, where in the series, Lynne Howard was shown working. Ray had a record number of about 1500 people on the ferry that day. They started coming over at about six o'clock in the morning. The Parish Council cleared the whole site to enable people to come down. They had additional toilet facilites, and they rigged up a grandstand on the hard. He's hoping that Howards' Way tourists will enable him to beat his record, but quite frankly, I doubt it somehow.

The picturesque location has formed the setting for other films down through the years. An old film called 'True as a Turtle' was made at Hamble in the early fifties, connected with the boats around the river, and was quite popular in it's day. There was also an 'Open Air' programme filmed recently. The presenter talked to Ray, but they didn't use any of it in the end. He took an organised party across the river and was filmed doing it. Some of the passengers were interviewed to see what they thought about the area. They were very impressed because coming from up North, they'd never seen anything like it before. It was filmed on a Sunday, at peak time with the maximum amount of yachts on the river. Ray tells me that it was just like trying to cross a motorway.

Ray would make an ideal character for the series, but was aghast when I suggested it to him.

"I wouldn't like to be associated with that sort of thing." he said. "The only thing I've been involved in recently is one of those 'Country Ways' programmes on TVS, presented by Jill Cochran. It was called 'Southampton Water in May'."

The Hamble River provides an ever-changing scene along its complete length, with the pretty upper reaches of the river giving way to picturesque villages along its banks and, finally, the hustle and bustle of the huge marinas as the river joins the Solent waters. It provides enormous scope for filming a wide variety of programmes, and perhaps we shall see more film makers sizing it up in the near future.

In the series, Ken Masters has bought into a powerboat

The busy Hamble Marina

yard. I wondered whether Ray would consider buying a powerboat from such a character in real life.

He tied up his old wooden ferryboat and laughed. "I wouldn't buy a powerboat at all!" He said.

Unlike most of the other residents, Ray is against change for change's sake, and is fighting against the housing developers who plan to build on the old airfield just outside of the village. But it's not only the dry land that is destined for change, as he explains...

"Down here on the river, we used to think that nothing could change, but marinas have been built, and they keep saying that there will be no more boats on the river, but Universal Shipyard has been sold, and already they're trying to make it into some sort of marina. There's already around about 3500 boats on the river, and that's quite enough, if you ask me!".

But back to Howards' Way. I wanted to learn more about Hamble's remarkable transformation into Italy, so I paid a visit to Mr Fletcher, the owner of Beth's restaurant in the heart of the village. Surely he could enlighten me.

The restaurant has been in existence since 1980, and was started up by a lady called Beth who was in partnership with Peter Nicholson, of the Camper and Nicholson company. It was originally three old cottages. Mr Fletcher has been the owner since 1984. Before asking about Howards' Way, I couldn't resist finding out a bit about some of the celebrities that seem to frequent the restaurant. The biggest 'megastar client' to munch through a meal recently was Duran Duran's Simon Le Bon. What's he like in real life?

"He's a very nice chap," said Mr Fletcher quite non-chalantly, as if this sort of client was an everyday occurrence. "He comes quite often. When Drum, his yacht, was on the river on trials, he used to visit quite often with his skipper, Novak. His family have also been here too. His brother, Jonathan, and his mother flew over for a birthday all the way from Florida. We did the party for them upstairs. Simon's just an ordinary chap. He likes playing about, going out with girls, and messing about on the water. In fact, that's

Beth's Restaurant in Hamble

The tea garden which became Italy for a short while

his main hobby. You don't spend a million pounds if it's not." (Well I wouldn't know, would I?) "He goes out with the lads on a Friday night, and probably has one or two too many sometimes, but we get on alright."

Chay Blyth, the round the world yachtsman, has also visited the restaurant. He was recently involved with the 'Cougar Marine/Virgin Records' attempt at the fastest Atlantic crossing with Richard Branson. Hamble seems to be a magnet for an incredibly wide variety of affluent people. Beth's even did a luncheon for the Prince of Japan recently.

In Hamble it seems that anybody who's anybody, belongs to the Royal Southern Yacht Club, on the quay. Being a somebody who's a nobody, as far as they're concerned, they refused to even talk to me, let alone let me in, without first holding a committee meeting to discuss it over a few G & T's. There seems to be so much red tape there that I would advise potential members to be careful they don't get tied up in knots!!

Back in Beth's, I asked Mr Fletcher how he was approached by the BBC for the Howards' Way scenes?

"They came down, saw my garden and said that it would be a perfect spot. It's very much a French/Italian type of garden. They thought that it would be ideal for the scene depicting Lynne Howard and Claude Dupont honeymooning in Italy. Surprisingly, they only needed to make a few minor changes, such as bringing in some plastic vines. The scene was originally planned to last for about six or seven minutes, but ended up being trimmed to thirty seconds. If you blinked, you'd have missed it!"

The filming at Hamble lasted a whole morning. The crew arrived the day before and spent practically the whole time constructing the set. Apparently, there were between forty and fifty people involved, including designers, set erectors, and the cast as well.

The road was closed off, but it was very well organised beforehand, and everybody in the village knew what was going on well in advance. If any of the residents had wanted

BBC tv

BRITISH BROADCASTING CORPORATION

TELEVISION CENTRE WOOD LANE LONDON W12 7RJ

TELEPHONE 01-743 8000 TELEX: 265781

TELEGRAMS AND CABLES: TELECASTS LONDON TELEX

9th October 1986

Mr Fletcher
'Beths'
The Quay
High Street
Hamble
Hants

Dear Mr Fletcher

Many thanks for all your help with the arrangements for filming "Howards' Way" at Beth's Restaurant. We had a most successful day and enjoyed working in Hamble. The scene filmed at 'Beths' will be shown on Sunday, 16th November in Episode 12.

Yours sincerely

pp Yvonne Alfer.
Mark Williams
Location Manager
HOWARDS' WAY

Mr. Fletcher was impressed by the BBC's thank you letter after the filming

to come down, they could have left their cars in the nearby car park and walked through.

The deliveries for the nearby pubs and restaurants were arranged so that they didn't co-incide with the filming, and so there were no difficulties. I enquired whether the local businesses were under the impression that the filming would boost trade in the area.

"People would be silly to believe that it was going to do them any good," said Mr Fletcher. "The BBC certainly didn't give me the impression that the restaurant was going to be 'featured' at all. They paid their location fee rate, and that was that. They were very professional in all respects. When they left the village it was perfectly clean, all the sand that they'd covered the road with, for effect, had been swept up. They worked very hard, and looked after everybody concerned. If anything, it was cleaner than before they arrived."

Mr Fletcher echoes much the same views as the other locals that I've spoken to, in respect of the finished series...

"It reflects, to a certain degree, the type of yachting fraternity that exists on the Hamble, but I thought that there was going to be a lot more sailing it it. It would have been better with less jumping into bed with everyone," he said.

I must admit, I didn't notice an abundance of permissive behaviour in the series myself, certainly not enough to cause Mary Whitehouse any consternation anyway. However, I was still interested in finding out exactly how the BBC had pulled off their 'Italian job'. . .

"Beth's was untouched because it looks like an old farmhouse anyway. They had an Italian priest walking down the street, and a chap on a Lambretta, with a girl sat on the back riding sidesaddle, as the Italians do, going up and down. I must admit that did get on people's nerves a bit. They filmed an awful lot more than what they showed and I think they were going to feature a lot more, but there was a very long scene in the same episode with Leo, which was about twenty minutes long, so I reckon they cut our scene to get that in. I think that Hamble is being used again in the

The restaurant was originally three cottages

The cosy interior of part of the restaurant overlooking the water

third series. I don't think it can be left out, it's such an integral part of the area. A lot of the real boat business is done over lunch here at Beth's, or in the Royal Southern Yacht Club."

Were Beth's customers interested in the fact that the restaurant was featured in the series?

"They couldn't give a monkeys really!" laughed Mr Fletcher, "as long as they get decent food and good wine they're not worried. One customer did ask me whether Jan Howard was really good looking though. . ." He paused. "I said she was okay with her make up on."

Commercialism, to an extent, can benefit an area, but does Mr Fletcher approve of thousands of sightseers invading the village?

"From my point of view, no, I don't approve, but for the small business people who have got to pass a winter in Hamble where almost no-one comes down, then, for their sakes I wouldn't grumble. But if I thought it was starting to get too commercialised I'd still rebel against it, because Hamble is a quiet place, and we already get more than enough tourism in from the river every summer anyway. I don't want to see candy floss and Howards' Way mugs everywhere.

But if it would make the council put a few more flowers on the front, and tidy it up then I might be a bit more lenient! I think the councillors could make it nicer. We have no hostilities or vandalism, so there's no reason at all why they couldn't put in a few blossoming cherry trees and some flower baskets. As far as people peering in my windows are concerned, that's okay, I'm used to it so I don't suppose a few more would matter, I normally just poke my tongue out at them anyway!".

Scene of the Wedding

The little church of St Leonard's, in Bursledon's aptly named Church Lane, was chosen for the setting of the wedding in the second series of Howards' Way, that took place between Lynne Howard and Claude Dupont. In real life, the church has a modern outlook, which is in complete contrast to the very olde worlde atmosphere created for the series. I asked the Reverend John Alderman how the church became a stage set;

"The first thing I knew was when I had a phone call from the location manager. He asked if he could pop down and have a chat about the possibility of filming in the church and it's surroundings. He talked about what the writers had in mind, and asked how we'd feel about it. I took all the details I could, and presented them to our Church Council. We decided to ask to see the script, to make sure that the wedding actually portrayed some sort of worship. Although it's only fiction, we wanted to ensure that it was right. So we stipulated a number of things. We wanted to find out how the whole concept of Christian marriage was going to be handled before we made our decision.

The scripts are a bit like gold dust, and it took a bit of wangling to get anything out of them. They were very anxious not to give away the plot, and we were sworn to secrecy. I don't think that any of us were viewers anyway, so it didn't have much significance. Mind you, we watched it when the church was on, of course."

St. Leonard's Church

The director wanted to create a romantic atmosphere in the church scenes, and did much of the shooting from a safety gantry erected in the clock tower alcove above the main door. From here, he produced some excellent shots, looking down on the congregation. Unfortunately, the aisle is rather narrow, and so they had to remove a row of seats on each side.

Lighting proved to be the biggest headache. It consisted mainly of two large tripod mounted lights, one on the Pulpit side, and one on the Vestry side. In addition, there were lots and lots of reflectors to bounce the light around. These things looked like tin foil placards. Two cameras were used. One in the high position, and one on a track outside for the shots of the bride and groom emerging.

It must have been a great opportunity for the Rev. Alderman to preach to his biggest ever audience, but the BBC had already engaged an actor to play the part of a Vicar. However, given the chance, would John have liked to officiate?

The narrow aisle was widened for the filming

The small church caused lighting problems

"I would have loved to have done, because I'd have done it quite differently. I did ask in jest, but there's no chance without an Equity card. We're very modern in our approach here, although, architecturally it may not look like it. In contrast, the BBC wanted the traditional 1928 service. They asked me to come along as technical consultant to make sure they got it right, and so I found myself learning lines along with the actors, because I hadn't conducted that service for five years or so. People always have the modern one, and that's our way of doing things.

The chap they 'wheeled' in to do the officiating was old, and several takes were needed before he got it right. It was a bit different to the way I would have taken it. It certainly wasn't the same as a 'normal' wedding occurring here on a Saturday in 1986."

The congregation in the scenes had to sit through their longest ever church service. It was all very unglamorous, and in the Vicar's words, 'incredibly boring'. It took two days to get the six minutes of footage required. Most of the congregation were the actors from the series, plus a few extras included as a gesture to some of the local people that had helped them.

The excitement caused quite a crowd of interested locals at the church gate who had wandered up from the village to ogle. Apparently, the BBC said, 'right stay there and ogle, and we'll film you doing it'.

The lighting for the inside of the church took ages to set up. The actual film sequences were quite quick, even though the 'vicar' kept getting his lines wrong. Although he had a book in front of him, he wasn't actually allowed to look at it, and because the service is in Old English, he stumbled over some of the words several times.

They kept their fingers crossed that one day of the two was going to bring good weather. Actually, during some of the outside shots towards the end of the outside day, the weather really did start to close in. Nobody would have guessed that the shots of the Bride and Groom coming out were filmed in light drizzle. It was amazing to see how the BBC 'doctored' the finished footage. They made us all completely unaware that it was any darker than first thing in the morning.

One question that I had always wondered about. . . Are on-screen weddings legally binding?

"Perhaps that's another reason why they didn't use me," said John Alderman, the Vicar. "If the actor used isn't a real Vicar then the wedding has no validity. They're very careful about which sections of the service they use. They always omit the parts where declarations are made.

We thought very carefully about whether the church should be used for a 'make-believe' service. We wanted to ensure that the characters weren't breaking any rules of Christian marriage, and living lives that were flagrantly immoral, or against what we, as Christians, stand for in the community. They included some marriage preparation in the script that we liked, of a conversation between the couple and the Vicar, strolling between the lychgate and the church door. That encouraged us to feel that the right sort of image was going to be presented. I had an image of TV moguls

Scene of the ceremony

coming here and riding roughshod over everything, but right from the very first contact, I've nothing but praise for them. They've become well-liked in the village from what I can gather."

I wondered what the Vicar thought of the series in general.

"The episode which included the wedding was the only one that I watched, and it looked very nice. I missed the rest of the episodes, the reason being that I have to go to work on Sunday nights!!"

I told John about the Southampton Tourist Board's plan to bring hordes of visitors to the area, and pointed out that, as the series had been such an outstanding success, St Leonard's was probably fair game as a tourist attraction.

"That's something else that we actually talked about, but incidentally, no one's ever arrived anyway!" he explained. "There was an initial feeling of unease amongst us, but the more we thought about it, the more we realised that we were wrong. We recognise that we have got a church that's attractive, and if we do get coachloads of people, then our Christianity might 'rub off' a little bit on them, which would be very pleasing. It certainly did on the cast, and I had some very interesting conversations with some of them while they were here."

I asked whether the Church Council would be happy to give the go ahead for something similar again, and learnt that there was in fact already something in the pipeline for the third series...

"We decided recently that we're going to refuse what they're requesting for the third series. They would like to do a funeral, using a few establishing shots of the church, from the churchyard, and then the traditional pictures of the lowering of a coffin into a grave, with the family gathered around. I've had two contacts with the location manager, and looked into various possibilities. At our council meeting we decided that we were happy about the establishing shots of the church and churchyard, assuming that the graves them-

Church of St. Leonard — through the trees

selves would be out of focus, to avoid identification. However, we were against the digging of a hole in the grounds.

We felt, as Christians, that we probably didn't have many objections ourselves about people laying cables across graves or disturbing the area, because we don't actually believe that anybody's under there. But, we are very aware that it could upset a lot of locals who's relatives are buried here. So we ended up thinking that, although as a council we would have voted 75-25 in favour, we felt that probably the village would want us to make the decision the other way.

I told the BBC that they couldn't use the churchyard, but the owner of the adjacent field would probably have no objections.

There's a big difference between filming a funeral and a wedding. Weddings are more neutral, and spiritual. Once you get into the realms of funerals and death, in an intangible way, you're on slightly dangerous ground."

I pressed the Vicar for more information on the forthcoming script, but either he wasn't telling, or he didn't know.

A true village church complete with lychgate

"I don't think it's Claude." he said coyly. "From what I can gather the series is about to take a brand new direction. I don't think they want to get close to reality. They seem to hype it up, week by week. If they don't have at least one traumatic incident an episode, then the thing loses it's edge, when in fact life isn't like that. There are definitely some new characters being introduced in the third series though, as far as I can make out. The impression that I got was that the series was going to be featuring more boating type episodes this time. Perhaps they're responding to public demand. Certainly most people around here would welcome such footage."

The super-smooth Claude Dupont character seems to lose his deep French accent directly the cameras are switched off.

"He's certainly from North of the Channel!" laughed John Alderman. "It's amazing how he puts it on, it was quite a shock. During the hours waiting for the lighting to be set up, we'd be chatting to the cast and so on, and he was VERY British. He certainly didn't speak like the 'Clodd' he was nicknamed. In fact, most of the cast are very approachable and very nice. They had no illusions of grandeur that I could see, which is just as well, I think."

Most small Parishes are always short of money, and so I guessed that, if the BBC had offered a fee, then it would have been very welcome. But what is the standard rate?

"It's £200 a day. We took advice and rang up the church office in London in advance to find out. They're dealing with this sort of thing all the time, and said that, in round figures, the fee we were offered was about right.

We were happy with our £400, and it was good fun, although it did begin to get boring towards the end of the second day. Everyone wanted to get finished, but the engineers were STILL sorting out the lights.

For me, the most interesting part was seeing the reality behind the glamour. It was great to see a bit of the actor's and actress's real lives. They were all busy attempting crosswords and reading the paper for hours on end, getting very bored. They seemed happy with intrusion of people for a chat to pass the time. They're just normal people like us, underneath it all."

Writing Howards' Way

Colin Haydn Evans was one of the writing team contributing scripts to the series. The first he knew about it was when his agent contacted him and asked, 'Do you know anything about sailing?' Colin admits that, even if the question had been, 'Do you know about Persian electric blankets?', his answer would still have been 'yes'. A writer has to eat!

That's how all new series start from the writer's point of view. Colin was told that it was a new series, set in a boatyard on the south coast. His agent put it in a nutshell; 'A nautical Dallas'. After agreeing, he was sent forth to read his 'bible'. This is a vast duplicated tome provided by the BBC that gives everything that the writer needs to know about the characters, settings, story developments, etc, together with reams of largely irrelevant material. Apparently it seems to take longer to read the infernal things than to actually write the script.

I wondered what came next...

"After thoroughly digesting all this material — even to the point of actually remembering the characters names, so as to look reasonably bright at the first script conference, you are ready to meet the producer and the script editor to be briefed on your particular episode."

Most of the time spent at such meetings seems to take the form of explaining how the current storyline bears little or no resemblance to the lengthy information just learnt;

"Often someone's thought of something better, and your

carefully prepared synopsis delivered prior to your visit is totally redundant!"

Usually scripts for other episodes have already been written, and the writer is faced with the unenviable task of trying to dovetail his or her work into what's already been accepted. Whatever happens though, I guessed that it must be exciting to be part of an enthusiastic new team;

"I am always surprised initially by the amount of enthusiasm generated by the first page of my script", explained Colin, "and the amount of depression generated by the last."

Some time before the final commissioned script is posted off, an enormous interwoven network of dates will have to be drawn up for the next year or so, just to ensure that everything runs smoothly.

"With Howards' Way, the background logistics were horrendous. Not only was it necessary to produce stories, scripts and characters, but boats as well. I pity the poor technical consultant to the series who must have wished he was half way round Cape Horn when it came to coaching sail-ignorant actors and actresses into pulling the tiller the right way, by lying on his stomach down the companionway, hissing instructions at a suitable sound level!"

I thought that it must be a relief when the first draft is sent off, and the job is almost finished, but it seems as if I was wrong;

"In television, 'first draft' really means 'you won't be off the phone much in ten days'. They are just building blocks towards the final script, and some hardly qualify as the sand in the mortar. In practice, they're just something for the script editor to mull over while he thinks about what he actually WANTS you to do. This can be anything from suggesting a total rewrite, to suggesting that you look for work on another series, or no series at all."

Howards' Way was, according to Colin, although I have heard stories to the contrary, conceived by producer Gerry Glaister, and the writer Allan Prior. These both have very impressive track records and, with John Brason, another skilled writer acting as script editor, there was no chance of anything going wrong in normal circumstances. A fact backed up by the audience appreciation accompanying the series. However, from a writer's point of view, it appears that it wasn't the easiest of series on which to work. Apparently the writing had to be very precise, and to a format so as not to risk losing any of the audience. It seems as if a lot of writer's just didn't make the grade, including Colin;

"I fell by the wayside after a single script. Good or bad didn't come into it in terms of my own capabilities, or the series requirements. It was just that our respective styles clashed, and I could only bridge the gap artificially. Some series allow more latitude, and so can accommodate a broader degree of interpretation. But in the case of Howards' Way, the scope was virtually non-existent. A highly professional team had conceived an equally professional format. Any writer that couldn't fit those requirements within his natural style was going to fall foul of the demands sooner or later."

It certainly seems to be a tricky business, and one of escalating difficulties as the characters interweave and the story gets more and more complex. However, it must beat having a real job, don't you agree?

Your Howards' Way Trail

Graham Shaw, from the Southampton Tourism and Conference Office, The Civic Centre, Southampton, SO9 4XF. Tel 0703 832504, has arranged some exciting Howards' Way weekends that have proved very popular with 'fans' from all over the country. They include a stay in one of Southampton's top class hotels, and the chance to meet one of the cast or crew of the series. However, if you prefer a more leisurely visit and are prepared to make your own accommodation arrangements then there's no reason why you couldn't head for 'Howards' Way country' under your own steam. If this appeals to you then you should find this specially designed Howards' Way trail useful. I've designed it in such a way that backtracking is kept to an absolute minimum, and all of the notable locations from the series are included. The tour, which begins and ends at the roundabout near junction 8 of the M27, is just ten miles long. It can be covered in a couple of hours, but if you really want to savour the atmosphere and enjoy a drink and a meal in the Jolly Sailor or the Fox and Hounds then you should allow a full day. It's fun to explore all of the locations that you've seen on the screen in depth, once you get there.

We begin by taking the first exit off of the roundabout. (You can't mistake it, as it has an enormous Tesco superstore right next to it). It's signposted Bursledon. Take the first right, at the bottom of the hill. This is the A3025, and is called Portsmouth Road. Off of this road, you want the second turning on the left. This is a sharp bend right next to Lowford Garage. Follow this around the corner and up the

Right at Hungerford Bottom

hill, then look for a right turn into Hungerford. You're now right in the heart of Howards' Way land!

The road branches at the bottom of the lane. Take the right fork and continue down the steep hill. In front of you is your first on-screen location, the Fox and Hounds/Lone Barn pub complex, run by Terry McEvoy and his wife. Why not stop for some refreshment? Terry will be only too pleased to recount his tales of the filming to you over a drink.

Afterwards, a short walk down the lane reveals a cottage on the right called Hunt's Folly. The garden of this was used for the scenes with Jan Howard's mother, although the cottage itself was not used. Since the filming, a lot of building work has taken place, but it is still recognisable, just.

On returning to your car, drive back up the hill and take the hairpin bend to the right into Kew Lane. Drive slowly, and keep your eyes right. The second house you come across is no less than the home of the Howards, Bondfield House. You should easily be able to recognise the porch, which

The Fox and Hounds at the foot of the hill

featured in the wedding scenes, (the Rolls Royce left from here carrying Lynne), and also the old conservatory on the left of the house. Don't stare too long though, and do be careful that you don't block the road. It's very narrow here.

Now follow the road along until you see a little grass triangle in the road with a telephone box on it. Bear right at this into Land's End Road. This is an exciting stretch as it houses both of the major locations. First of all, you will see a sign up for the Elephant Boatyard, which as we all know now, is better know these days as the Mermaid Yard. There is a footpath that affords a better view, but Tom Richardson, the real life owner doesn't welcome intrusions; you have been warned. You will get a better view anyway from the Jolly Sailor pub, which is a matter of yards further down the road on the left. It is reached by a steep winding path. It's best to walk around to the entrance that faces the river, as this provides the opportunity to take some pictures from the jetty and pontoon that extends from the pub. This is perhaps the most famous panorama of all, taking in the Elephant

Hunts Folly

Bondfield House as seen from the road

The Elephant Boat Yard as seen from the Jolly Sailor

The rear of the Jolly Sailor

Boatyard, the Jolly Sailor, and the forest of masts on the river. You'll have seen it on your screens countless times.

Once back in the car, proceed down to the bottom of Land's End Road, and turn around. If the weather's fine, the bench on the grass bank provides a fantastic view of the river, and is an excellent place to take a picture. However, if you do decide to stop for any length of time, do ensure that your car doesn't obstruct the turning circle there.

When you're ready, drive back up the road and bear right. You'll soon find yourself heading down a steep narrow hill, but don't worry, it's one way traffic! The road soon levels out, and you approach a junction. Turn left into Church Lane, then left again, and you'll see St Leonard's Church in front of you. The scene of the wedding between Lynne Howard and Claude Dupont. You can park just past the lychgate on the left, but keep well in to the verge.

From the church, carry on along the lane, and turn right on the steep incline. This takes you, after half a mile or so, to Bridge Road. You emerge right next to the Swan pub/

A nice spot to pause for a moment

St. Leonard's Church

restaurant. If you want a last look at the Jolly Sailor and the 'Mermaid Yard' before leaving 'Tarrant', then leave your car in the Swan car park, and walk the few hundred yards to Bursledon Bridge.

The next stage of our trail takes us to Hamble, the South Coast's yachting mecca, and stage set for many Howards' Way scenes. From Church Lane, turn left and proceed up the hill (Bridge Road). You'll soon be back at the roundabout that you begun from. Take the first exit into Hamble Lane. Ensure that you keep to the right hand lane. The left one is reserved exclusively for Tesco's superstore traffic. Keep to this road, and after several miles you will find yourself on the outskirts of Hamble. The village's links with aviation can be clearly seen, (perhaps this prompted the Tom Howard-aircraft designer idea) and on your right there is an old 'Gnat' aircraft, as used by the Red Arrows, and built here. Also, almost directly opposite, is a pub called the Harrier, named after the jump-jet which was also built in the area.

But I digress, back to Howards' Way. . . Opposite Hamble

Bursledon Bridge offers a good view of the Hamble River

A Gnat aircraft built in the area

Motors, you will see Hamble Service Station. Perhaps if you decide to fill up here, you might be served by Leo, as this was the garage that he was filmed working in, in the series.

The road winds it way onwards until it comes to the old village of Hamble. Slow down and bear right, entering the one-way system into the village next to the Lloyds bank. The Italian scene that I mentioned in an earlier chapter was filmed down this very road. The 'set' started opposite the King and Queen pub, with Portland House which sported gaily painted shutters for a day or so, but has now reverted back to it's dull former self. Beth's restaurant is on the left, and you can peep through the wrought iron gates and see where Claude and Lynne were sitting, under the grapevines in 'pseudo-Italy'. It's amazing what the camera can do, isn't it? Opposite is the Compass Point Chandlery, which was transformed into a delicatessen.

Park on the Hamble Parish Council's foreshore, and after having a look at the Royal Southern Yacht Club, on the quay, where Lynne Howard worked in the series, follow the signs

Hamble Service Station

The author in Hamble assisting with some photographic equipment!

Ray Sedgewick — aboard the Warsash ferry

and walk to the Hamble/Warsash ferry. This is a little motorized rowing boat, run by a friendly fellow by the name of Ray Sedgwick. He's a goldmine of information on the series if you get him talking. The trip across the river from Hamble to Warsash costs, at the time of writing, just 20p each way. Children go for half fare. The trip is great fun, and it offers a totally different perspective of the river, presenting an ideal opportunity for some memorable photographs of the nautical vista, from a yachtsman's eye view.

On the way across, ask Ray to point out the Victoria Rampart jetty. This became New York Harbour in the scene where Lynne completed her Atlantic crossing in the Barracuda. It stretches the imagination a bit doesn't it? When you alight from the ferry, turn right and walk along the riverside track, past the car park. On the right you will see the Victoria Rampart offices themselves. These were pressed into service for the external shots of Ken Master's chandlery, and Jan Howard's boutique.

A yachtsman's view

When you return to your car, you have no option but to follow the one way system up the hill and out of Hamble village. This takes you past Hamble Manor to the junction with School Lane. If it's a nice day then Hamble beach can be reached by turning left and following the road. It's a pretty bleak, grubby place though, overlooking Fawley Oil Refinery. If you don't fancy it, then turn right, and follow the road to the junction. Turn right again here, (this brings you back to where you started) and then left into Satchell Lane. Look for the sign for Port Hamble. This is where the money is. There must be millions and millions of pounds floating in the big marina. Quite a few scenes were filmed out on the pontoons, and Laser, the makers of the Flying Fish, are based here.

Further up the road is the home of Barracuda's designer, Tony Castro. He lives in Rio House. It is signposted, but unfortunately the old farmhouse is not visible from the road. After reaching the end of Satchell Lane, turn right into Hamble Lane. This will take you back to the roundabout where it all started.

I hope you've enjoyed your trip, and had some fun peeping into a little bit of England where fact meets fiction on the waves, where a hamlet suddenly becomes the talk of the Nation, and a stretch of water, renowned the world over for it's yachting connections became, for a while, THE REAL HOWARDS' WAY.

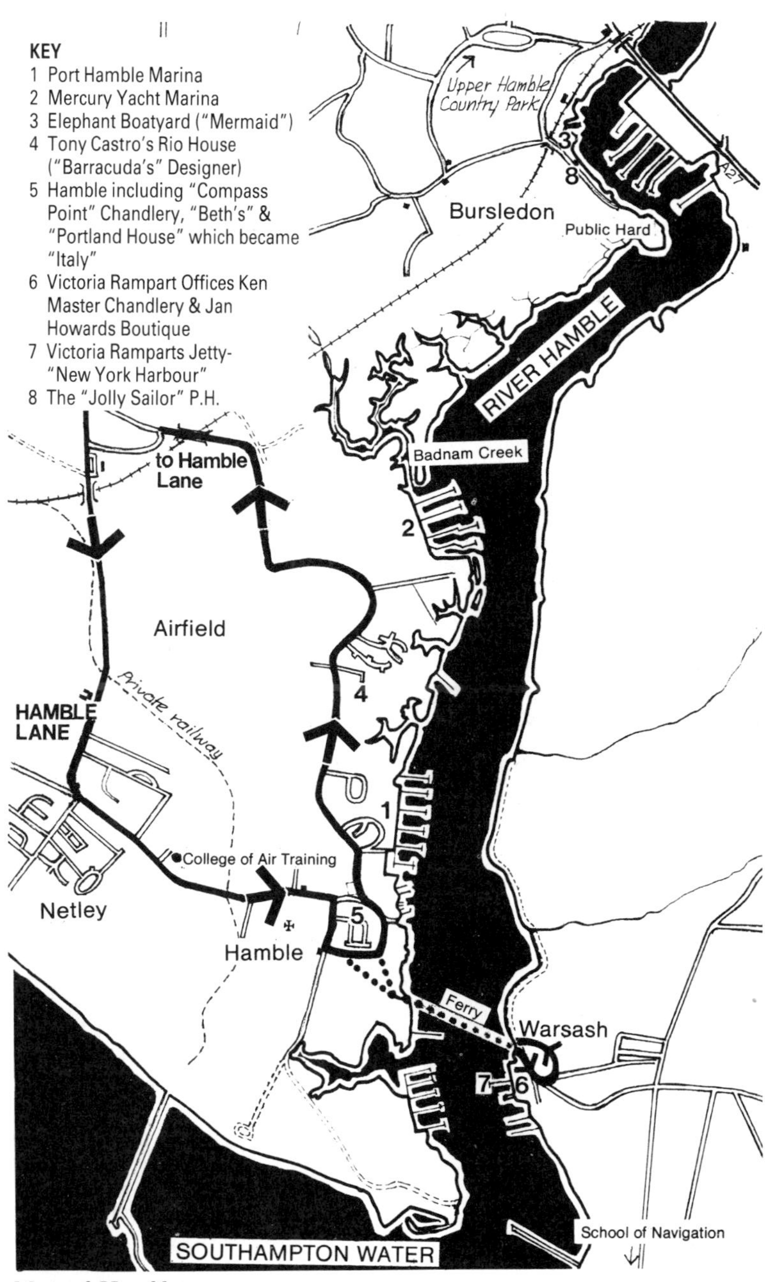

Map of Hamble

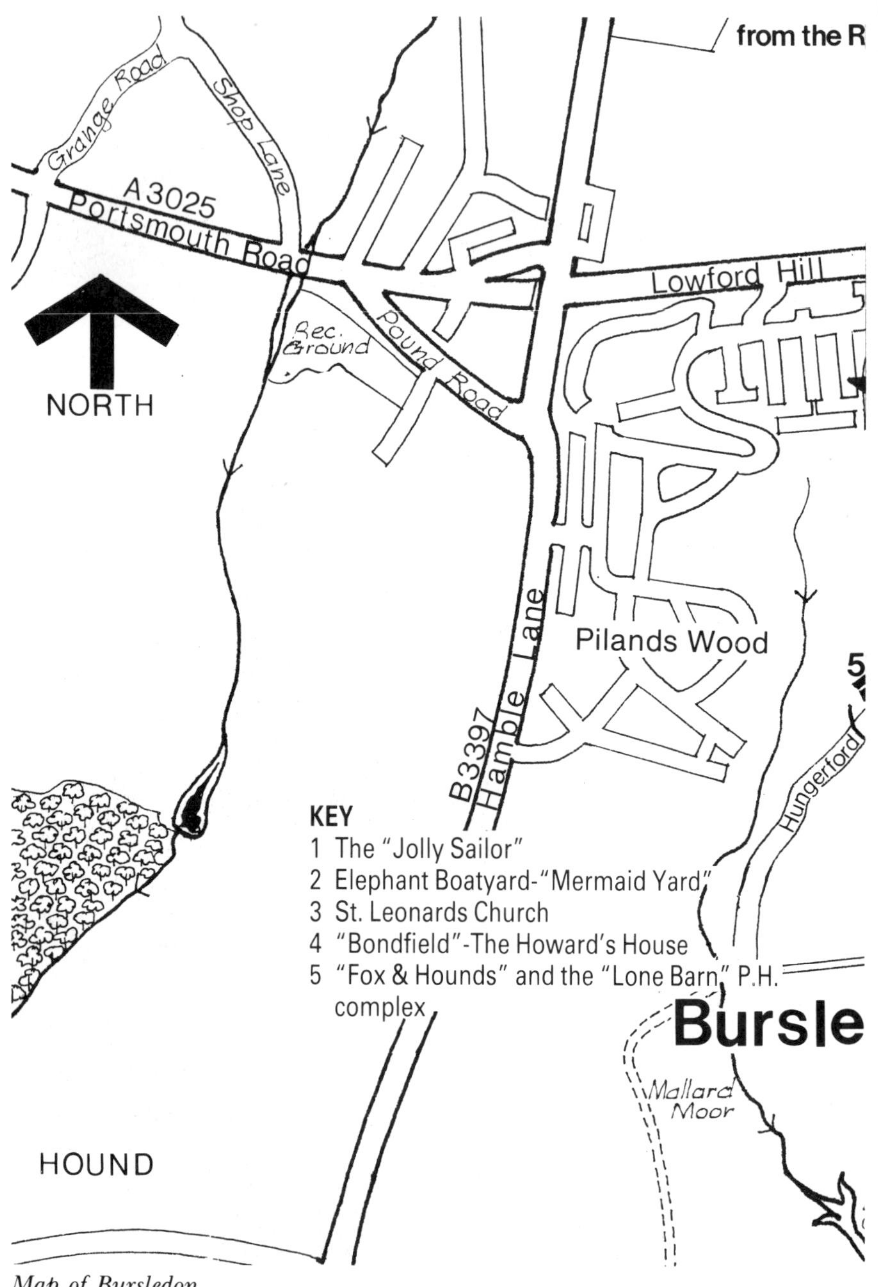

Map of Bursledon

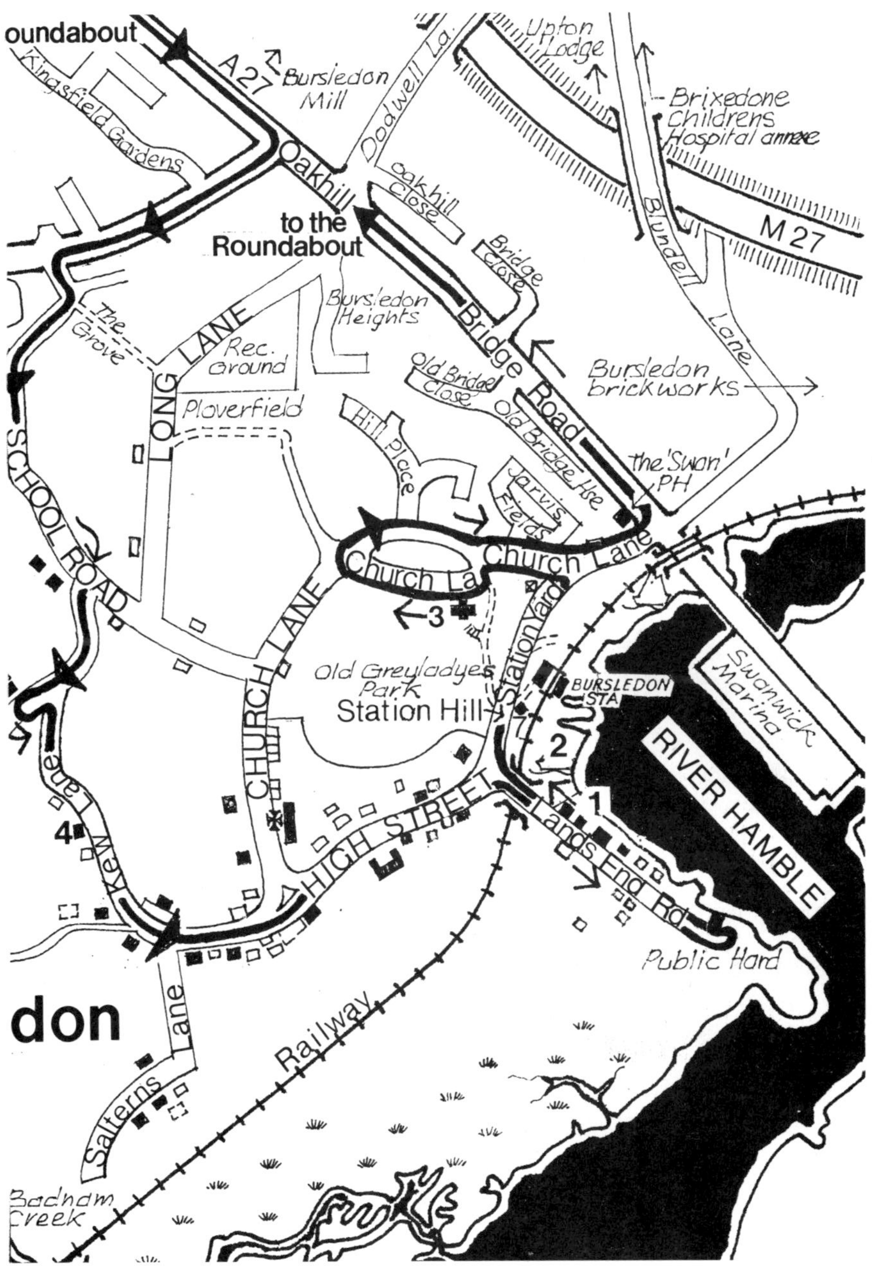
oundabout
Kingsfield Gardens
A27
Bursledon Mill
Dodwell La.
Upton Lodge
Brixedone Childrens Hospital annexe
M 27
Oakhill
Oakhill Close
to the Roundabout
Bridge Close
Blundell Lane
The Grove
LONG LANE
Rec. Ground
Bursledon Heights
Bridge Road
Bursledon brickworks
Old Bridge Close
Old Bridge Hse
Ploverfield
Hill Place
Jarvis Fields
the 'Swan' PH
SCHOOL ROAD
Church La
Church Lane
3
CHURCH LANE
Old Greyladyes Park
Station Hill
Station Yard
BURSLEDON STA
Swanwick Marina
RIVER HAMBLE
2
1
4
Kew Lane
HIGH STREET
Lands End Rd
Public Hard
don
Railway
Salterns Lane
Badnam Creek

Clive Brooks

As a professional author, Clive Brooks has contributed to an exceptional variety of publications, both in Britain and America. Subjects have ranged from children's stories, through travel and technical articles, to hi-tech musical features, working from his base in Southampton where he owns his own tuition and recording centre, the Sound Workshop.

Always interested in film production, he has taken some time out to produce this exciting journey around a village where fact and fiction co-exist.

David Ellery

Originally from London, David Ellery is a photographer with many years experience. During this time his assignments have been wide and varied. From pictures for local newspapers, through promotional material for chain stores and cosmetic companies, to photographs for women's magazines.

Ellery's philosophy is not to rely heavily on special effects, but instead to take time and trouble to set up shots carefully.